Mark Twain Laughing

MARK TWAIN
LAUGHING

HUMOROUS ANECDOTES
BY AND ABOUT
SAMUEL L. CLEMENS

EDITED, WITH AN INTRODUCTION,
BY PAUL M. ZALL

The University of Tennessee Press / Knoxville

Copyright © 1985 by The University of Tennessee Press / Knoxville.
All Rights Reserved. Manufactured in the United States of America.
Cloth: first printing, 1985; second printing, 1986;
            third printing, 1987.
Paper: first printing, 1987; second printing, 1997.

Frontispiece illustration by Eucalyptus Tree Studio.

Library of Congress Cataloging in Publication Data
Main entry under title:

Mark Twain laughing.

     Bibliography: p.
     Includes index.
     Twain, Mark, 1835–1910—Quotations. 2. Twain, Mark,
1835–1910—Anecdotes. 3. Humorists, American—19th
century—Biography. 4. Authors, American—19th century—
Biography. I. Zall, Paul M. II. Twain, Mark, 1835–1910.
PS1303.M344 1985   818'.402   84-29169
ISBN 0-87049-464-3 (cl.: alk. paper)
ISBN 0-87049-544-5 (pbk.: alk. paper)

for Rosy & James

Contents

Mark Twain: Voice of America Laughing

These anecdotes and sayings by and about Mark Twain have been selected to represent the building blocks of his comic art. These discrete, self-contained bits and pieces have lain scattered widely in his notes, letters, books of all kinds as well as in newspapers, magazines, and private collections. In the aggregate they gave shape to America's comic masterpieces, not just the celebrated stories, sketches, and novels but the colossal comical creation of Mark Twain himself.

In his own time every preacher, teacher, public speaker collected just such stories and sayings as are compiled here. In that oratorical age writing was meant to be read aloud, literature meant to be memorized for individual performance more for fun than for profit. On the range cowboys starved for literature read the labels on the cook's tin cans until they knew them by heart.[1] One would sing out a key word and the others would chant the remainder in unison. They could always tell a tenderfoot because he did not "know his cans."

Twain's generation shared a communal pleasure in the English language, memorizing passages from the Bible, scenes from Shakespeare, sometimes circuit-riders' sermons or stump-speakers' orations, even congressional debates. President Lincoln was notorious for peppering his speeches with stories he would clip from comical books and humor columns of the daily newspapers, which would then reprint his version of them in a round robin of quipping and clipping. Mark Twain enjoyed the same relationship with the press, shared even the same stories with the president.

Mark Twain's material differed from others' in the way he used

1. Ray Allen Billington, *America's Frontier Culture* (College Station: Texas A&M Univ. Press, 1977), 60.

it. He would use the anecdotes to interrupt the smooth flow of stories until, as in *Innocents Abroad,* the anecdotes themselves take over and become the story. The bits of dialog helped him experiment with the sounds of Americans talking, which were reproduced with highest fidelity in *Huckleberry Finn.* Later entries in his notebooks show experiments with the maxim, which in its passion for compression represents the antithesis of the leisurely, rambling anecdote that Twain had stamped as distinctively American. For those intrinsic reasons, these bits and pieces have been worth compiling.

But an added benefit emerged from assembling them in order of the earliest date I could find for each one. They reflect Mark Twain responding to a cultural revolution that has only recently been apparent to historians.[2] Everyone knows that at the opening of his career the nation's bounty seemed as boundless as her borders and her energy. At the close of his career that energy was being dissipated in the drive for industrial and imperial supremacy worldwide. For reasons still not quite clear, the nation's traditional oratorical culture gave way to an urgent concern with print-oriented literacy. Twain's maxims, for instance, reflect this new urgency in their concise, precise wit.

Such anomalous sketches as the scatological "1601" or the mock lecture on onanism are included to show that, though he may have changed with public taste as a professional was bound to do, Mark Twain retained a private attachment to the more primitive humor that had once carried the Wild Humorist of the Pacific Slope into hearts all over the world. After his death, cronies and self-styled bosom companions tried to replay that old-time humor, but samples of their efforts also included here make them sound like Livy Clemens swearing: They get the words right, but they don't know the tune (see **418**).[3] It is too bad so many casual readers know Mark Twain only through what other people say. That is why the aim of the present work is to let Mark Twain speak for himself even if only in bits and pieces, for these bits and pieces

    2. Lawrence W. Levine, "William Shakespeare and the American People," *American Historical Review* 89 (1984): 34–66.
    3. Unless noted, stories in this introduction are based on texts printed below in chronological order and listed in the index.

enable us to reconstitute both the words and the music of America laughing.

In his old age he told fifteen-year-old Frances Nunnally that the truth of his achievement could be found in the May 1909 issue of *Harper's Magazine.* He referred to the interview he had given to Archibald Henderson, who concluded by trying to explain Mark Twain's unprecedented acclaim not only at home but overseas.[4] Henderson said that Sam Clemens himself embodied the spirit of the whole nation, the self-made man in a homemade democracy the whole world admired. As writer and lecturer he had created Americans' image of themselves, which they tried to live up to and which Europeans would recognize anywhere: irreverent, independent, bold, brash, big-hearted, exuberant, and awfully noisy, a boisterous people always laughing, usually at themselves.

When Sam Clemens himself was fifteen he was working as a journalist, writing fillers or whatever was needed for his brother Orion's succession of midwestern small-town newspapers. At sixteen, he published his first story nationally in the Boston comic weekly, *The Carpet-Bag.* It was a sketch, "The Dandy Frightening the Squatter," about an eastern dandy passenger on a steamboat showing off before female passengers at a landing. He approaches a slight-appearing lounger and threatens him with a pistol: "Found you at last, have I? You are the very man I've been looking for these three weeks! Say your prayers! . . . You'll make a capital barn door and I shall drill the keyhole myself!" The tight-lipped lounger disarms the dandy and tosses him into the river to the applause of the onlookers.

The sketch contained nothing to distinguish it from others floating on the crest of the national newspaper fad for stories about the wild frontier. Then, traveling as a journeyman printer who could also play reporter, Clemens started moving with the frontier, even taking time out to study piloting the Mississippi. As he traveled, he assumed the role of a naive frontier bumpkin commenting on the manners of creeping civilization then infesting St. Louis and New Orleans. As Thomas Jefferson Snodgrass,

---

4. Vol. 118 (May 1909): 948–55, later incorporated into his *Mark Twain* (London: Duckworth, 1911). Clemens's advice to Frances Nunnally is in an unpublished letter of 29 April 1909, Huntington Library accession number HM 48482.

he put on the comical pose of the stage Yankee of his youth. Originally a character in plays whose native mother wit would foil the cultured city folk, the Yankee became westernized as traveling actors also moved west with the frontier,[5] until ultimately he became a mongrel mixture of the naivete and chutzpah inherent in the personality of Mark Twain, a western Yankee.

Thus by the time Sam Clemens reached the West Coast, Thomas Jefferson Snodgrass had been left behind. In his place rose Mark Twain to absorb the westerners' energy, the idealism thinly layered on violence, but especially the exhilaration in exuberant talk, talk, talk—the real sound of America on the move. As he said, "Americans drop into anecdotes as soon as they get a little acquainted."[6] He caught them in the act even as Mark Twain himself evolved from a naive tenderfoot, an easy target for tall tales and put-ons, into a ruggedly independent anecdotal con artist in his own right.

His boisterous style and comical sketches hardly set him apart from the legion of competing comic columnists—of whom Bret Harte is perhaps still remembered. They all delighted in the kind of eccentric characters Twain favored: The grizzled miner who refuses to hunt Indians because he hadn't lost any, or the dispirited Devil in Hell who finally exclaims: "The trouble with you Chicago people is that you think you are the best people down here; whereas you are merely the most numerous." Mark Twain assimilated the sound of the West in the process of telling stories—not merely the vocabulary or word order but the actual voice. He did this not by artificial phonetic spelling of the "phunny phellow" school of comic journalism but by studying the sounds of speech.

One of the editors who worked on *Following the Equator* described the result as "plain American-English": "He sees like an American, thinks like an American, feels like an American, reasons like an American, is American, blood and bone, heart and head."[7] Mark Twain himself published an 1880 essay on the

5. See David Grimsted, *Melodrama Unveiled: American Theater and Culture 1800–1850* (Chicago: Univ. of Chicago Press, 1968).
6. *Mark Twain's Notebook*, ed. Albert Bigelow Paine (New York: Harper, 1935), 267.
7. Quoted in Hamlin Hill, "Mark Twain: Audience and Artistry," *American Quarterly* 15 (1963): 30.

American language, distinguishing it from British English then the manner of speech among "the educated handful" in this country, who were trying to impose it upon "the vast uneducated multitude."[8] The point was to validate the spoken American language as distinct from the artificial literary standard imported from Great Britain.

The essay reflects the same concern evident in his correspondence to get the language down just right: "I amend dialect stuff," he told his friend William Dean Howells, "by talking & talking & *talking* it till it sounds right."[9] The considerable art behind that practice is evident also in notebook entries over the years. In series they sound like cocktail party conversation overheard: *"There's* sap for your pine-apple." *"Agreed* with him?— Got him downstairs on the ice." "I always do that when I drink claret." "I *did* eat some corn, but darned if I et the half of *that."*[10]

In this way Mark Twain reconstituted the sound of Americans laughing at themselves—the exaggerated boisterous yawp of the West, the twang of the Midwest, the maddening rumination of the New Englander, the drawl of the southerner. He captured the music as well as the words of southern conversation, for instance, which Allen Tate described as "not going anywhere, it is not about anything" but "the people who are talking, even if they never refer to themselves."[11] Sam Clemens's mother is overheard: "And such a sight as he was—there he sat, almost stark naked— not a thing on but a pair of spectacles—and one of *them* was broke and you could see him right through it."

Besides recording the life around him with dramatic immediacy, Mark Twain's art made use of literary resources also, amply analyzed in the recent two-volume study by Alan Gribben, *Mark Twain's Library.*[12] To the large number of books in his library must

8. "On the American Language," *Writings of Mark Twain* (Hartford: American Publishing, 1899), 20: 405–409.
9. *Mark Twain–Howells Letters,* ed. H.N. Smith and W.M. Gibson (Cambridge, Mass.: Harvard Univ. Press, 1960), 1: 26.
10. *Notebooks and Journals,* ed. Frederick Anderson, et al. (Berkeley: Univ. of California Press, 1975), 2: 343, 344, 345.
11. "A Southern Mode of the Imagination," *Studies in American Culture,* ed. Joseph J. Kwiat and Mary C. Turpie (Minneapolis: Univ. of Minnesota Press, 1960), 101.
12. 2 vols. (Boston: G.K. Hall, 1980).

be added the myriad newspapers and magazines as well as books he consulted casually. In an obscure collection, *Literary Anecdotes* compiled by E.H. Barker in 1852, one item describes the trick later used to uncover Huck Finn's masquerade as a girl:

> Two thieves, disguised as country-girls, obtained admittance at a farm-house, which they intended to rob. In the course of the evening, the farmer began to entertain suspicion of their sex. To settle the point, he tossed into their laps the shells of some nuts he had been cracking. The pretended females immediately closed their knees to prevent the shells from falling through, forgetting that women never do so, because their petticoats accomplish that purpose for them. (1: 282)

From such raw anecdotes came additional ingredients for Mark Twain to shape into the sound of America laughing.

The process of transformation can be seen even in the famous story of the jumping frog when it is compared with the same tale as told in two earlier newspaper versions. Mark Twain's version appeared first in the New York *Saturday Press* for 18 November 1865. It is told not by the author but by Simon Wheeler when Mark Twain asks him if he knows about a Reverend Leonidas W. Smiley.

> "Reverent Leonidas W. H'm, Reverent Le—— well, there was a feller here once by the name of Jim Smiley, in the winter of '49 — or maybe it was the spring of '50 — I don't recollect exactly, somehow, though what makes me think it was one or the other is because I remember the big flume warn't finished when he first come to camp; but anyway he was the curiosest man about always betting on anything that turned up you ever see. . . ."[13]

By contrast, the anonymous version in the Sonora *Herald* for 11 June 1853 was headed "A Toad Story" and began thus: "A long stupid looking fellow used to frequent a gambling saloon. . . . One day he came in with an important air, and said 'I have got

---

13. This is the text Mark Twain revised in 1869 to emphasize the sound of Simon Wheeler's monologue; *Early Tales and Sketches,* ed. E.M. Branch and R.M. Hirst (Berkeley: Univ. of California Press, 1981), 2:677. The earlier versions are in Oscar Lewis, *The Origin of the Celebrated Jumping Frog of Calaveras County* (San Francisco: Book Club of California, 1931), Appendix, [31–34].

a toad that'll leap further than any toad you can scare up.'" In similar fashion the anonymous version in the San Andreas *Independent* for 11 December 1858 opens: "Joe B., formerly of Calaveras County, was, is, and always will be a sport. He bets on every game. . . ."

He would transform his own published work as well. In the practice common then, he would publish his stories in the popular press and then in book form. Publishing in newspapers and magazines paid the initial reward. The books provided additional profit, especially if, as in Mark Twain's case, they were sold by subscription as ornately bound, illustrated, deluxe volumes. But the truly successful humorist reaped the best rewards on the lecture circuit, an oratorical medium.

As Mark Twain traveled the circuit he would commit a selection of about fifty anecdotes to memory, then vary them to fit each occasion or audience, in this way refreshening the stock by transforming each anecdote as the occasion warranted until some of them emerged wholly new. Speaking one day about the old ram story, he said he had memorized it and then "it began to undergo changes on the platform and it continued to edit and revise itself, night after night" until after a dozen years he looked at a printed version and could hardly read it aloud.[14]

In his own day Mark Twain was more popular as a speaker than as a writer. He was able to pay off debts of his failed publishing business by undertaking a lecture tour around the world to resounding acclaim. His anecdotes were of course more congenial to speaking than to reading. Even when he read from his books he would adapt them to the lecture platform. Rehearsing daily, he would polish anecdotes or passages no matter how many times he had performed them previously, adapting both substance and style to new requirements. And as he traveled around the world he would pick up new material. As his own experience broadened from frontier to global scope, so his anecdotes and sketches became more varied in substance and style. As the substance became more genteel, the style became more literary than vernacular.

Eyewitnesses concur that he retained the self-deprecating yet

14. *Mark Twain in Eruption*, ed. Bernard DeVoto (New York: Harper, 1940), 217.

brash manner of frontier story tellers, adding immeasurably, however, to his platform presence by pacing, timing, gestures, and
particularly the manipulation of his voice that typified his art.
Most obvious idiosyncrasy was his sometimes maddening habit
of drawling out his remarks—with long pauses, signified in print
by dashes. California editor Noah Brooks who had been an intimate of Abraham Lincoln and of Mark Twain too described the
latter's performance as "unique and novel": "His slow deliberate
drawl, the anxious and perturbed expression of his visage, the
apparently painful effort with which he framed his sentences, and,
above all, the surprise that spread over his face when the audience roared with delight."[15]

J.M. Barrie remarked how this stage manner had become so
habitual with the older Twain that he used it in conversation:
"His voice fell and he turned his face away from me and his one
hope seemed to be that I should not catch his meaning. He always appeared to be pained in a gentle lovable way if his listeners
smiled, and it almost broke him up if we laughed."[16] This deadpan delivery must have become second nature. William Rideing,
editor of the *North American Review,* knew him thirty years and
in all that time never knew him to laugh.[17] Clemens himself suggested that Mark Twain's writings seldom made him laugh.[18] Someone once suggested he never smiled, either, because—like George
Washington—he did not wish to show his bad teeth.

The *London Spectator* (October 1903) lauded that deadpan
manner as part of his art, "the unconscious, matter-of-fact way
in which he habitually strikes false intellectual notes, the steady
simplicity with which he puts the emphasis of feeling in the wrong
place . . . and so glides into sarcasm or caricature, while seeming
to pursue . . . the even tenor of his way."[19] The slow, agonizing
drawl, part of the understatement characterizing his method, was

15. *Century Magazine* 57 (Nov. 1898): 98.
16. *Who Was Sarah Fielding?* (London: Clement Shorter, 1917), 7–8.
17. *Many Celebrities and a Few Others* (Garden City: Doubleday, Page, 1912), 154.
18. *Mark Twain's Notebook,* ed. Paine, 151.
19. Quoted in Paul Fatout, *Mark Twain on the Lecture Circuit* (Bloomington: Univ.
of Indiana Press, 1960), 181.

crucial to the role he played, as crucial as the slipping into the brilliant aside ("Familiarity breeds contempt—and children") or the antiquated joke ("Tiger on front porch eating station-master! Wire instructions") or the profound lament ("Principles have no real force except when one is well fed").

On the stage Mark Twain might be talking about the exuberant verbosity of old miners, pilots, commercial travelers, but he was playing the role of a crusty old Yankee, a western Yankee who drags out a story with a punishing stammering drawl. An eye-witness describes Mark Twain's telling a London audience about a magical mountain:

> "It is so cold that people who have been there find it impossible to speak the truth. I know that's a fact (here a pause, a blank stare, a shake of the head, a little stroll across the platform, a sigh, a puff, a smothered groan), because—I've—(another pause)—been—(a longer pause)—there myself."[20]

As he used to say about his own hero Artemus Ward, "It's un-kind to report him. There's more in his pauses than in his words."[21]

The lecture platform provided still another dimension, inter-action with a live audience accustomed to actively listening if not actually participating in the creative process. "The other night at Meriden," he wrote home to his wife from one lecture tour, "I struck upon an entirely new manner of telling [the jumping frog story]. Without altering a single word, it shortly becomes so absurd that I have to laugh myself."[22] He describes the epiph-any: "Last night I got to one particular point in it three times before I could get by it and go on. Every time I lifted my hand aloft and took up the thread of the narrative in the same old place the audience exploded again and so did I." Each great perfor-mance must have meant a mutual renewal like an old-fashioned revival meeting.

20. *Mark Twain*, 104.
21. Paul Fatout, *Mark Twain Speaking* (West Lafayette, Ind.: Purdue Univ. Press, 1978), 45. George Ade said of Twain, "He knew how to make one second of silence outweigh a hundred words"; *One Afternoon with Mark Twain* (Chicago: privately printed, 1939), 10.
22. *Love Letters of Mark Twain*, ed. Dixon Wecter (New York: Harper, 1949), 41.

He did not lecture formally but rather read aloud from his published works, adapting them of course to time, to place, and especially to audiences. Even when reading from the best-known works, he would distill them, then rehearse aloud no matter how many times he had read from them before, as each time meant a new performance. He studied the art of humorous story telling as seriously as he studied the American language: The humorous story indigenous to America "fools along & enjoys elaboration" as opposed to the kind of wit that is vivid and brief as though shot out of a pop-gun.[23] His classic essay "How to Tell a Story," in *Youth's Companion* for October 1895, concluded: "To string incongruities and absurdities together in a wandering and sometimes purposeless way, and seem innocently unaware that they are absurdities, is the basis of the American art" in the ageless tradition of seemingly artless art.[24]

Mark Twain's humorous story telling relies on anecdotal interruptions and digressions to upset our expectations of a straightforward narrative flow, or a well made plot that moves straight ahead. Instead, he prescribed that "narrative should flow as flows the brook down through the hills and the leafy woodlands, its course changed by every bowlder,"[25] using imagery of a flowing stream remarkably similar to Robert Burton's in his role as Democritus Junior prefacing the *Anatomy of Melancholy* back in the seventeenth century: "As a River runs, sometimes precipitate and swift, then dull and slow; now direct, then windingly; now deep, then shallow; now muddy, then clear; now broad, then narrow doth my style flow"[26] — a style designed to create the illusion of spontaneity. The focus was on the process rather than the product of creation. Like Allen Tate's southern conversation, Mark Twain's little stories were "not going anywhere, not about anything" but Mark Twain's mind in motion.

In the last twenty years his stories became more literary than oratorical. Two of his favorite sketches, in fact, came from other authors' minds. One was about the officious clergyman christen-

23. *Notebooks and Journals*, 3: 162, 449–50.
24. *How to Tell a Story and Other Essays* (Hartford: American Publishing, 1900), 7–15.
25. *Autobiography*, ed. A.B. Paine (New York: Harper, 1924), 1: 237.
26. Ed. A.R. Shilleto (London: G. Bell, 1896), 1: 30–31.

ing the infant of a socially prominent family before a socially prominent congregation. Hoping to impress them, he develops an elaborate prophecy for the child, proclaiming the day when this child
would be another Caesar, Napoleon, Hannibal, Alexander, "or
both in one, and become master of the universe." Then, preparing for a grand finale, he whispers to the parents, What is his
name? "Mary Ann, is it?" That one came from Bram Stoker, now
better known for his *Dracula.*

Mark Twain's other favorite, the one he told in concluding his
farewell address to London in 1908, was from Dana's best-selling
Two Years Before the Mast. It tells about the frivolous captain of
a coast-hugging sloop in the dried apple and kitchen furniture
trade who hails every ship in sight. A majestic Indiaman plows
by "with course on course of canvas towering into the sky." Our
little captain squeaks, "Ship ahoy! what ship?" And the reply
thunders in a deep bass, "The *Begum of Bengal,* 123 days out
from Canton—homeward bound with sugars and spices, frankin-
cense and myrrh! What ship is that?" The little captain, vanity
crushed, humbly squeaks back, "Only the *Mary Ann*—14 hours
out of Boston, bound for Kittery Point—with nothing to speak
of!" In this valedictory, deriving from a best-selling book known
to his audiences worldwide, Mark Twain played the role of per-
former rather than creator.

This is not to suggest that the creative spark had gone out.
Back in New York later that same year he roasted his dear friend
Andrew Carnegie with the story of the Hartford prosecutor named
Clarke, infamous browbeater of witnesses, who gets his comeup-
pance from a washerwoman, plaintiff in a rape case. He badgers
her: "If one may take so preposterous a thing as that seriously,
you might even accuse me [of rape]. Come now, tell me, suppose
you should wake up and find me lying beside you? What would
you think?" "I would think," says she, "that I'd had a miscarriage."
The Wild Humorist of the Pacific Slope was alive and well on
the banquet circuit among friends.

He had traveled a long way in forty years, but so had his audience changed, too. Complained one colleague: "The old-time
audience demanded a speech of not less than 2 hours . . . and
expected 3. The audience of today grows restive after the first

xx Mark Twain Laughing

hour and is better pleased with 45 minutes."[27] In meditating on this phenomenon, Lawrence W. Levine suggests some of the complex causes lie in the "influx of millions of non-English-speaking people" represented by "more than one thousand foreign-language newspapers and magazines published in the United States by 1910," along with a parallel growth in literacy, which undermined "the pervasive oral culture that had created . . . an audience more comfortable with listening than with reading."[28]

Whatever the cause — social, cultural, technological — the effects are apparent in Mark Twain's conversion to the art of the maxim, both his own and the maxims of others. From his neighbor and sometime collaborator, Charles Dudley Warner, came the one about politics making strange bedfellows and the most famous maxim misattributed to Mark Twain, "Everybody talks about the weather but nobody does anything about it." From his friend Carnegie came, "Put all your eggs and in one basket and watch that basket." In 1894 he used forty maxims for chapter headnotes in *Pudd'nhead Wilson*. Three years later he doubled the number in *Following the Equator.* His notebooks filled up with one-liners as he tried to distill the wisdom of the ages. He told Archibald Henderson that this represented a change in career objective: Earlier he had been content to make people laugh; now he wanted to tell them truth.[29]

He was now trying to do for Americans what George Bernard Shaw and Oscar Wilde were doing for their countrymen, articulating a cynical, jaundiced view in polished pop-gun wit, appealing to an impatient audience preferring epigrams to arguments, humor to rhetoric. He was not alone in this respect, for humor columns throughout the nation were also favoring maxims with similar aim if not of similar quality. Typical of the humor columns were: "Home is where the mortgage is" or "Silence gives content" versus Mark Twain's "Man is the only animal that blushes. Or needs to."

The avalanche of maxims all but buried the raconteur of old.

27. Will Clemens, ed., *DePew Story Book* (London: F.T. Neely, 1898), 111–12.
28. "William Shakespeare and the American People," 57.
29. Henderson, *Mark Twain*, 99.

His prescription of "a minimum of sound to a maximum of sense"[30] subverts the whole idea of the raucous, rambling anecdotes that had reconstituted the voice of America laughing. It was thanks to his earlier interest in language and in the nature of wit and humor that he was able to make the transition. The basic structure of a maxim is the same as that of a joke—a build line followed by a punch line: The difference is that both elements are contained in the maxim's one sentence, as in defining a classic as "a book which people praise [build line] and don't read [punch line]."

In undercutting received opinion or cultural dogma, he was following a tradition lost in antiquity, but which surfaced in the Middle Ages in popular debates between wise King Solomon and a raunchy German peasant, Marcolphus. Whether Mark Twain did it consciously or not, he assumed the role of the wily Marcolphus, whose function was to show the underside of Solomon's sententious wisdom. In the sixteenth-century verse version, the king speaks twenty-three proverbs and the peasant counters with twenty-three "converbs" about the pleasures and penalties of whoring; e.g., "He that a hoor for hym self kepeth / She often another in his sted taketh / Whan his money no longer wyll endure."[31]

As in Twain's work, the Solomon-Marcolphus tradition featured anecdotes as well as proverbs. A prose version also published in the sixteenth century displays an excremental vision that could have been a prototype for "1601": In one episode, the king, fed up with Marcolphus's heckling, banishes him. Marcolphus takes up residence in an abandoned oven. Coming upon the oven, the king opens the door to find Marcolphus curled up backwards: "Wherefore liest thou thus?" From the depths of the oven, Marcolphus reminds him that the king had ordered him never to show his face, and so he is only following orders.[32]

30. Caroline T. Harnsberger, *Mark Twain at Your Fingertips* (New York: Beechhurst Press, 1948), 259.

31. *Sayinges or Prouerbes of King Salomon* (London: Richard Pynson, [1530?]), STC 22899.

32. *The Dialogue or Communying between the Wise King Salomon and Marcolphus*, ed. E. Gordon Duff (London: Lawrence and Bullen, 1892), 31–32.

From this ageless tradition come Mark Twain's private stories about the physician uncertain whether the short patient has piles or a sore throat, and the bride whose tummy is found imprinted with an advertisement for a patent medicine guaranteed to cure the clap. In public, however, though he played the private eccentric, his duty was to articulate the spirit of the age, the communal sense of humor. In Louis Budd's view, "Twain created the role of court jester to self-esteem, blending argument and ridicule to make man humbler before himself without realizing he had been insulted."[33] By the close of his career the New York *Times* estimated that he was quoted in common conversation more often than any other American, including Ben Franklin and Abe Lincoln.[34] What could be a better sign of success for the voice of America laughing?

Many of his maxims, even those he adopted from others, as the one on doing something about the weather, have taken on the force of proverbs. Just as anecdotes that had once been tied to Joe Miller attached themselves to Mark Twain's name, so maxims by others also became attached despite his disclaimers — as his assertion, "The remark attributed to Disraeli would often apply with justice and force: 'There are three kinds of lies: lies, damned lies, and statistics.'" Many of those attributed to him by later writers seem beyond authenticating, especially the now proverbial remark about not appreciating his father till turning twenty-one: "When I was a boy of 14, my father was so ignorant I could hardly stand to have the old man around. But when I got to be 21, I was astonished at how much he had learned in 7 years."

By registering the name "Mark Twain" as a trademark, he could control publication of anecdotes by him but those about him were considered public domain even while he lived. Unauthorized biographies sprouted early in his career and spread in proportion to the broadening of his fame at home and abroad, often no more than anecdotes clipped from the newspapers. Mark Twain threatened to sue Will Clemens, no kin, for publishing such an unauthorized work but never took it to court, leaving it to circulate as a sourcebook for other unauthorized biographies. Thus he who

33. *Our Mark Twain* (Philadelphia: Univ. of Pennsylvania Press, 1982), 223.
34. Ibid., 4.

had built a career on literary hoaxes, most notably the figure of Mark Twain himself, ultimately became the victim of hoaxes himself. He who lives by the hoax dies by the hoax?

In changing the course of his career from the rambling raconteur, the Wild Humorist of the Pacific Slope, to the quixotic quipper of quotable maxims he risked losing his public. His ideal recipe for the maxim was "a minimum of sound to a maximum of sense." Yet he had conditioned his public's ear to a maximum of sound. Consider the implications of the story he tells about addressing his daughter's classmates at Bryn Mawr:[35]

She gave him strict orders not to embarrass her this time, and so he offered to share with the young ladies a serious poem he had written. "'Now, ladies, I am going to read you a poem of mine'—which was greeted with bursts of uproarious laughter. 'But this is a truly serious poem'—only to be greeted with more uproarious laughter.

"Nettled by this misunderstanding, I put the poem in my pocket, saying, 'Well, young ladies, since you do not believe me serious I shall not read the poem' at which the audience almost went into convulsions of merriment." The Wild Humorist of the Pacific Slope had done his work too well. Fifty years of programmed preconceptions are hard to overcome.

As a professional, the nonpareil of his era, Mark Twain had to adapt to changing times, changing audiences, becoming in the course of events the national emblem of nostalgia for better times that never were, while trying to keep in tune with what was happening. In another commencement address, to Frances Nunnally's graduating class at Miss Tewksbury's school just outside Baltimore, he sounds less like the Wild Humorist of the Pacific Slope than a westernized Oscar Wilde: No stories, just rapid-fire quotable one-liners.

"First, girls, don't smoke—that is, don't smoke to excess. . . . I never smoke to excess—that is, I smoke in moderation, only one cigar at a time. Second, don't drink—that is, don't drink to excess. Third, don't marry—I mean to excess." That was his last public performance, June 1909. But the next month, at home, he

35. Henderson, *Harper's Magazine* 98 (1909): 951.

showed the Wild Humorist was still alive and well in Connecticut still recording the sound of America laughing at ourselves: "I came in with Halley's comet in 1835. It is coming again next year, and I expect to go out with it." Then, as in the old days, turning the laugh: "The Almighty said, no doubt, 'Now here are these two unaccountable freaks; they came in together, they must go out together.'" And they did.

A Note on Editorial Method

Mark Twain's estate had been planned with care. A board of trustees retained firm control over the trademark and all published and unpublished works, carefully doling out permission to print or reprint them. They could do little, however, to control the flow of stories and sayings attributed to him, often fancifully, by old acquaintances or distant relations. Opie Read, for instance, who had enjoyed his own repute as "The Arkansas Traveler," spent his last year reminiscing about his adventures with Mark Twain for the Chicago *Daily News*. Total strangers added their bits handed down from generations like family heirlooms, now willingly given up to the shrine of Mark Twain, god of American humor.

Apocryphal stories and sayings, staples of jokebooks, soon mingled with folklore, as the story about the New Yorker accusing Missourians of being too provincial and Mark Twain replying, "Nobody in New York knows anything about Missouri, but everybody in Missouri knows all about New York." Attaching Mark Twain's name refreshed such old jokes but obfuscated his proper role in American humor. They are included here only to contrast with the authentic stories or sayings intrinsically and to show what commercial jokemasters have done to a national monument. I have tried to include notes commenting on their authenticity as well as providing information about Mark Twain's own achievement.

In selecting the entries my chief aim has been to represent his comic art through the bits and pieces that created it. My requirements were that the entries fall under at least one of some half-dozen loose criteria: (1) Preference was given to those that were self-contained even when extracted from a larger literary unit. (2) As distinct from literary exposition, description, or commentary, highest priority was given to dramatic "events," complete with setting, characters, and action but especially with lifelike and lively language. (3) In trying to use some measure for what is "humorous," I have preferred entries referring to ridiculous ambiguity of language, behavior, or appearances as well as incongruity of image and absurdity of idea. (4) With very few exceptions I have preferred briefer to longer versions even though this meant sacrificing such personal favorites as the Blue Jay yarn, rationalizing that these were readily available in standard textbooks. (5) I have accordingly included such long pieces as "1601," representing a less publicized side of Mark Twain precisely because these have not been generally available in so handy an edition as this aims to be. (6) Ultimately, my aim has been to provide a useful book for reliable reference as well as casual, enjoyable reading. The notes have meant threading the fine line between pedantry and pleasantry, but I have risked the former in favor of utility, clarifying allusions or terms along with short references to general and specific sources given in complete form in the bibliography. Entries are indexed by topic and subject.

Acknowledgments

In the notes I have indicated the source for each entry, trying as often as possible to restore the earliest published or written version. As a result I have had to rely heavily on the Mark Twain Papers being published by the University of California Press, which has gracefully granted permission to reprint excerpts. At the same time, I have enjoyed full cooperation from the staff of the Mark Twain Papers project at the Bancroft Library under direction of Robert H. Hirst, who generously granted me permission to consult unpublished material there.

Otherwise, my work has been done entirely within the marvelous halls of the Huntington Library, former repository of the Mark Twain Papers, which yet retains a magnificent collection of manuscript and print material by and about Mark Twain. My strongest support has come from a former assistant curator of the papers while they were here, Edwin H. Carpenter. There is no way to acknowledge how much his friendship and counsel have contributed to my work over thirty years. Others contributing to the present project represent resources of the Huntington also seldom acknowledged, such visiting scholars as Robert Adams Day,

Michael Lofaro, and Michael Timko, a never-failing source of aid, criticism, stimulation, compassion, along with the low-profile catalogers Mary Jones, Kathy Martin, Linda Williams, and Lee Zall. I would also like to thank Theresa Flores and Jeanne Gee.

The following are special acknowledgments, as required by the permission grantors:

The previously unpublished maxims by Mark Twain are © 1986 by Edward J. Willi and Manufacturers Hanover Trust Company as Trustees of the Mark Twain Foundation, which reserves all reproduction or dramatization rights in every medium. They are published here with the permission of the University of California Press and Robert H. Hirst, General Editor of the Mark Twain Project at Berkeley.

Specified material from pp. 23, 6–7, 44, 60, 330–331, 347, 348, frontispiece in MARK TWAIN IN ERUPTION, Edited by Bernard DeVoto.
Copyright 1922 by Harper & Row, Publishers, Inc.
Copyright 1940, 1968 by The Mark Twain Company.
By permission of Harper & Row, Publishers, Inc.

San Marino, California   P.M.Z.
Summer 1984

Abbreviations

AL   *American Literature*

AL Laughing P.M. Zall, *Abraham Lincoln Laughing* (Berkeley: Univ. of California Press, 1982)

ALR   *American Literary Realism*

ET&S   Samuel L. Clemens, *Early Tales and Sketches,* ed. E.M. Branch and Robert Hirst (Berkeley: Univ. of California Press, 1979)

Fatout   Samuel L. Clemens, *Mark Twain Speaking,* ed. Paul Fatout (Iowa City: Univ. of Iowa Press, 1976)

Gribben   Alan Gribben, *Mark Twain's Library,* 2 vols. (Boston: G.K. Hall, 1980)

MT   Mark Twain

MTE   Bernard DeVoto, ed., *Mark Twain in Eruption, Hitherto Unpublished Pages about Men and Events* (New York: Harper, 1940)

MTJ   *Mark Twain Journal*

MTP   Mark Twain Papers, Bancroft Library, Univ. of California, Berkeley

NAR   *North American Review*

N&J   *Notebooks and Journals,* ed. Frederick Anderson, et al., 4 vols. (Berkeley: Univ. of California Press, 1975–)

Mark Twain Laughing

The Anecdotes

1851

1. At the fire on Thursday morning, we were apprehensive of our own safety, (being only one door from the building on fire) and commenced arranging our material in order to remove them in case of necessity. Our gallant *devil,* seeing us somewhat excited, concluded he would perform a noble deed, and immediately gathered the broom, an old mallet, the wash-pan and a dirty towel, and in a fit of patriotic excitement, rushed out of the office and deposited his precious burden some ten squares off, out of danger. Being of a *snailish* disposition, even in his quickest moments, the fire had been extinguished during his absence. He returned in the course of an hour, nearly out of breath, and thinking he had immortalized himself, threw his giant frame in a tragic attitude, and exclaimed, with an eloquent expression: "If that thar fire hadn't bin put out, thar'd a' bin the greatest *confirmation* of the age!"

Hannibal *Western Union,* 16 Jan. 1851; *ET&S* 1: 62. This earliest extant publication of MT's work features the printer's devil, Jim Wolfe, who will appear in a later popular story, "Jim Wolfe and the Tom-Cats."

1856

2. Night before last I stood at the little press until nearly 2 o'clock, and the flaring gas light over my head attracted all the varieties of bugs which are to be found in natural history, and they all had the same praiseworthy recklessness about flying into the fire. They at first came in little social crowds of a dozen or so, but soon increased in numbers, until a religious mass meeting of several millions was assembled on the board before me, presided over by a venerable beetle, who occupied the most promi-

3

nent lock of my hair as his chair of state, while innumerable lesser dignitaries of the same tribe were clustered around him, keeping order, and at the same time endeavoring to attract the attention of the vast assemblage to their own importance by industriously grating their teeth. It must have been an interesting occasion — perhaps a great bug jubilee commemorating the triumph of the locusts over Pharaoh's crops in Egypt many centuries ago. At least, good seats, commanding an unobstructed view of the scene, were in great demand; and I have no doubt small fortunes were made by certain delegates from Yankee land by disposing of comfortable places on my shoulders at round premiums. In fact, the advantages which my altitude afforded were so well appreciated that I soon began to look like one of those big cards in the museum covered with insects impaled on pins.

The big "president" beetle (who, when he frowned, closely resembled Isbell when the pupils are out of time) rose and ducked his head and, crossing his arms over his shoulders, stroked them down to the tip of his nose several times, and after thus disposing of the perspiration, stuck his hands under his wings, propped his back against a lock of hair, and then bobbing his head at the congregation, remarked "B-u-z-z!" To which the congregation devoutly responded, "B-u-z-z!" Satisfied with this promptness on the part of his flock, he took a more imposing perpendicular against another lock of hair and, lifting his hands to command silence, gave another melodious "b-u-z-z!" on a louder key (which I suppose to have been the key-note) and after a moment's silence the whole congregation burst into a grand anthem, three dignified daddy longlegs, perched near the gas burner, beating quadruple time during the performance. Soon two of the parts in the great chorus maintained silence, while a treble and alto duet, sung by forty-seven thousand mosquitoes and twenty-three thousand house flies, came in, and then, after another chorus, a tenor and bass duet by thirty-two thousand locusts and ninety-seven thousand pinch bugs was sung — then another grand chorus, "Let every Bug Rejoice and Sing" (we used to sing "heart" instead of "bug"), terminated the performance, during which eleven treble singers split their throats from head to heals, and the patriotic "daddies" who beat time hadn't a stump of a leg left.

It would take a ream of paper to give all the ceremonies of this great mass meeting. Suffice it to say that the little press "chawed up" half a bushel of the devotees, and I combed 976 beetles out of my hair the next morning, every one of whose throats was stretched wide open, for their gentle spirits had passed away while yet they sung — and who shall say that they will not receive their reward? I buried their motionless forms with musical honors in John's hat.

Letter to Annie Taylor, from Keokuk, Iowa, dated "Sunday, May 25th" 1856 and reprinted by Fred W. Lorch, "MT in Iowa," *Iowa Journal of History and Politics* 27 (1929), 422–24. Lorch identifies "John" as John W. Kerr, a fellow printer's apprentice. Annie Taylor was a Keokuk girl then away at school, Iowa Wesleyan University, Mount Pleasant.

3. [Thomas Jefferson Snodgrass reporting on his first visit to the theater in St. Louis, 18 October 1856:] I reckon there was nigh onto forty thousand people setting in that theatre — and sich another fannin, and blowin, and scrapon, and gigglin, I hain't seen since I arrived in the United States. Gals! Bless your soul, there was gals there of every age and sex, from three months up to a hundred years, and every cherubim of 'em had a fan and an opery glass and a — tongue — probably two or three of the latter weapon, from the racket they made. No use to try to estimate the oceans of men and mustaches — the place looked like a shoe brush shop.

Presently, about a thousand fellers commenced hammerin on the benches and hollerin "Music," and then the fiddlers laid themselves out, and went at it like forty millions of wood sawyers at two dollars and a half a cord. When they got through the people hollered and stamped and whistled like they do at a demercartic meeting, when the speaker says something they don't understand. Well, thinks I now I've got an old coarse comb in my pocket, and I wonder if it wouldn't take them one-hoss fiddlers down a peg and bring down the house, too, if I'd jest give 'em a tech of "Auld Lang Syne" on it. No sooner said than done, and out come the old comb and a piece of paper to put on it. I "hem'd and haw'd" to attract attention, like, and commenced Doo-doo-do-doo — do-doo. "He, he he," snickered the gals. "Ha, ha, ha," roared the mustaches. "Put him out." "Let him alone." "Go it, old Coun-

try." "Say, when did you get down?" and the devil himself couldn't
a hearn that comb. I tell you now, I was riled. I throwed the comb
at a little man that wasn't saying nothing and ris right up. "Gentlemen and Ladies," says I, "I want to explain. I'm a peaceable
stranger from Keokuk, and my name is Thomas Jefferson Snodgrass—" "Go it, Snodgrass." "Oh, what a name." "Say, old Country, whar'd you get that hat?" Darn my skin if I wasn't mad. I
jerked off my coat and jumped at the little man and, says I, "You
nasty, sneakin degenerate great grandson of a ring-tailed monkey, I kin jest lam—" "Hold on there, my friend, jest pick up your
coat and follow me," says a military lookin gentleman with a club
in his hand, tappin me on the shoulder. He was a police. He took
me out and after I explained to him how St. Louis would fizzle
out if Keokuk got offended at her, he let me go back, makin me
promise not to make any more music durin the evening. So I let
'em holler their darndest when I took my seat, but never let on
like I heard 'em.

Keokuk *Post*, 1 Nov. 1856; rpt. Fred W. Lorch, "MT in Iowa," 439–
40.

4.   [To the boarders gathered around the coal fire after breakfast on a brisk Sunday morning, Mr. Doodle tells a yarn as he
is interrupted by Mr. Jonas Cabbage, here abbreviated to "No.
2," distinguishing him from his father "Cabbage Senior."] An old
farmer had a big buck ram which would invariably chase him out
of one of his fields every time he went into it; and one day, as
he stood on the stile, bowing and smirking with excessive polite-
ness to some ladies passing by, the ram took a stand about twenty
yards behind him, and then measuring his distance and his target with a knowing eye, he darted forward, planted his head with
tremendous force just beneath the old man's short coat tail, and
sent him heels over head into a hog-wallow on the other side.
The old gentleman swore vengeance; and after thinking over divers
plans, he at last hit upon this one: He got an old wooden chair
seat and filled one side of it with sharp-pointed nails, allowing
them to project about half an inch. Went to the meadow—knelt
down near the stile, and placed the board against his wounded

seat of honor, but through some mistake, turned the nail side next himself.

No. 2. Oh! ha! ha! ha!—that was a good one!—tell us another.

Others. Dry up—dry up—the yarn isn't finished.

Doodle. In about three seconds the old enemy sent his head against that board like a battering ram, driving the nails home so effectually that the old man says he felt like a sieve for three weeks afterwards.

Everybody. Ha! ha! Served him right.

No. 2. Yes, served him right, but then what the devil did he turn the nails *in* for?

Keokuk *Post,* 18 Nov. 1856 as a letter from Cincinnati from "L," attributed to MT in *ET&S* 1: 382–86.

5. [Mr. Toploftical continues the conversation:] Well, that reminds me of an old ram that once got into a man's cellar one dark night. The servant maid went down and come up frightened to death at the *devil* she had seen. Then the old man went down, and finally the oldest son, all seeing the devil. Then they sent for the parson, and he went down, wrapped in his cloak, and kneeling on the ground, began to pray. The ram came up behind and butted him clear across the cellar. "Save yourselves, brethren," said he, "for the devil's got my cloak."

Doodle looks vacantly at Pottery; Pottery looks at the elder Cabbage, and the younger vegetable gazes into everybody's faces. There's a damper on that conversation! No man knowing whether the anecdote was intended to be funny or serious; they are afraid to risk a laugh, so the company assumes a grave air, and one by one they leave, until finally the room is deserted—a conversation murdered by a pointless anecdote.

Ibid., 386.

6. [Thomas Jefferson Snodgrass reporting on the terrible Cincinnati winter:] After a spell, the City Council concluded to try ther hand at relievin the sufferin community. They laid in a stock of coal, and advertised to sell cheap, and to poor devils only. But it was curus to see how the speckalation worked. Here's a instance:

A indigent Irish woman—a widow with nineteen children and several at the breast, accordin to custom, went to the Mayor to get some of that public coal. The Mayor he gin her an order on the Marshal; the Marshal gin her an order on the Recorder; Recorder sent her to the Constable; Constable sent her to the Postmaster; Postmaster sent her to the County Clerk, and so on, tell she run herself half to death, and friz the balance, while she had sixteen places to go yet, afore she could git the coal. But that is only just half of the little circumstance. You see that Widder had been trotting after Recorders and Postmasters and sich for considerable more'n a good while—and the Curoner's jury that sot on her scraped up the orders she'd got and sold 'em to the paper mill at three cents a pound, clearin about four dollars and a half by the speculation.

Keokuk *Post,* 10 Apr. 1857; Lorch, "MT in Iowa," 449.

7. [Commenting on the compulsion of Democrats to turn out for every election:] The only man I ever knew who could counteract this passion on the part of Democrats for voting, was Robert Roach, carpenter of the steamer Aleck Scott, "plying to and from St. Louis to New Orleans and back," as her advertisement sometimes read. The Democrats generally came up as deck passengers from New Orleans, and the yellow fever used to snatch them right and left—eight or nine a day for the first six or eight hundred miles; consequently Roach would have a lot on hand to "plant" every time the boat landed to wood—"plant" was Roach's word. One day as Roach was superintending a burial the Captain came up and said:

"God bless my soul, Roach, what do you mean by shoving a corpse into a hole in the hill-side in this barbarous way, face down and its feet sticking out?"

"I always plant them foreign Democrats in that manner, sir, because, damn their souls, if you plant 'em any other way they'll dig out and vote the first time there's an election—but look at that fellow, now—you put 'em in head first and face down and the more they dig the deeper they'll go into the hill."

San Francisco *Examiner,* 30 Nov. 1865; rpt. *ET&S* 2: 313–14.

1865–1867

The next ten entries are from notebooks MT kept during Jan. 1865–Jan. 1867. These are from the edition by Frederick Anderson, et al., in the series "Works of Mark Twain," published by the University of California Press. References are to volume and page.

8. Man in San F[rancisco] jumped lot & built house on it propped on low pins—hogs used to congregate under it & grunt all night—man bored holes in floor & his wife poured hot water through—hogs struggling to get out hauled the house down the hill on their backs & the lot was re-jumped by its proper owners early in the morning.

1: 78–79. This probably combines two events a decade apart: About 1851 a local bachelor named Henry kept hogs who ruined his house in this way; William R. Gillis, *Gold Rush Days with MT* (1930), 242–45. In 1863 MT covered a celebrated trial for the San Francisco *Call* (30 Aug.) in which a man whose house slid down upon a neighbor's property claimed the land.

9. Scene—Woods in Cal[ifornia] in early times—one-armed man finds man tied up to tree—says "They tied you up, did they?"—yes. "You're tied tight, are you?—yes. Can't get loose?—No—"Then by ——— I go [indecipherable word] you myself."

1: 83. Descendants of this hoary anecdote still circulate, as in *Playboy's Complete Book of Party Jokes* (1972), 124–25, where the raunchy cowboy comes upon a pioneer woman whose wagon was burned, husband killed, children abducted, and who had been left staked to the ground to perish. With more modern compassion, he tells her: "Well, ma'm, it looks like today just ain't gonna be your day," as he unbuckles his gunbelt.

10. Lincoln said, "You like McClellan—h——l on dress parade—no account in action."

1: 130. Though MT recorded this in Hawaii during the summer of 1866, it had been circulating among Lincoln's surving cronies the previous winter. The story is about a beautiful cock, a consummate strutter who was "not worth a dam in a fight"; *AL Laughing,* 56.

11.   Kanaka fondness for big funerals—fellow died for one.

Ibid. Another well-known anecdote also attributed to Lincoln spoke of an unnamed general: "If General ——— had known how big a funeral he would have had . . . he would have died years ago"; *AL Laughing,* 90.

1866

12.   In gale, man sent up to saw off topmast—blew all teeth out of saw. What yr lat & longitude? I was in same storm, 3 degrees to eastward—teeth blew aboard of my ship.

1: 158. In the notebook, this is headed "Lie."

13.   Sailor ordered to steer on a star—got on another—said he had passed *that* star & got up to another.

1: 161.

14.   Man took plaster for wife's abdomen—druggist said formed of 2 Greek words, meaning stop both outlets to body—must be cut in two—asked in morning for result—"Ab well enough, but domen blowed plaster all to hell [.]

1: 164.

15.   Rise early—it is the early bird that catches the worm. Don't be fooled by this absurd saw. I once knew a man who tried it. He got up at sunrise & a horse bit him.

1: 184. In one of the still unpublished notebooks in the Mark Twain Papers, Bancroft Library (notebook 42, p. 68), one entry adds to "healthy, wealthy, and wise": "too wise to do it again"; Gribben, 1:243.

16.   Water taken in moderation cannot hurt anybody.

1: 189.

17.   Man in Humboldt declined to go out & hunt Indians—said he hadn't lost any.

1: 293.

1867

18.   Felix McClusky, another San Franciscan, and an innocent, matter-of-fact man, is in Washington, and holds, or did hold, an office there which did not require that its occupant should know more than thirty-five or forty men ought to know — he had charge of the heating apparatus of the Capitol. They say that he had a steam engine in his department which he was very proud of, and was always showing it and expatiating upon it to visitors. One day one of these asked him what its capacity was — how many horse-power?

"Horse-power, h——l!" he says, "it goes by steam!"

Alta California, 13 May 1867.

19.   And that reminds me about an anecdote concerning General [W.T.] Sherman, who is now a resident of St. Louis. On his march down toward Atlanta, he constantly astonished the rebels with the facility with which he restored the railroad bridges they destroyed at his approach. They would annihilate a bridge just before he arrived, and the next morning there it was again, just as it had been before they touched it. At last a light dawned upon them. The original plans for the bridges had all been furnished from Cleveland, Ohio, and before Sherman started he took those plans, had each bridge duplicated in all its timbers and iron work, took the pieces in a "shook" state on his trains, and so, when he found a bridge gone, he had nothing to do but get its mate out of the freight cars, bolt it together, and put it up. This thing worried the rebels a good deal when they found it out.

One day they proposed to destroy the Dalton tunnel, to hinder Sherman's march, but an exasperated Confederate said: "What in the nation's the use? That d——d old Sherman's prob'ly fetched another one along with him from Cleveland!"

Ibid. Except for the fact that the mass-produced bridge parts were made in Nashville rather than Cleveland, this was the popular anecdote of Civil War times, perpetuated in such schoolbooks as John D. Champlin, Jr., *Young Folks History of the War for the Union* (1881), 472. It could have been in reference to this anecdote that Gen. Sherman said

"I WAS GRATIFIED TO BE ABLE TO ANSWER PROMPTLY, AND I DID. I SAID I DIDN'T KNOW."
—Life on the Mississippi, Ch. 6

Cartoon courtesy of Watterson, copyright © 1983 by the *Mark Twain Journal*.

at Delmonico's in 1888: "That story lost nothing in the telling, Clemens"; John Drew, *My Years on the Stage* (1922), 159.

20.   *Jim Townsend's Tunnel.* He was a stockholder in the "Daly" mine, in Virginia City, and he heard that his Company had let a contract to run a tunnel two hundred and fifty feet to strike the ledge. He visited the premises, and found a man starting a tunnel in very near the top of a very sharp hill. He said:

"You're the man that's got the contract to run this tunnel, I reckon?"

"Yes."

"Two hundred and fifty feet, I hear?"

"Yes."

"Well, it's going to be a mighty troublesome tunnel—and expensive."

"Why?"

"Because you've got to build the last hundred and sixty-five feet of it on trestle-work—it's only eighty-five feet through the hill!"

Alta California, 26 May 1867.

21. The steamer Ajax encountered a terrible storm on her down trip from San Francisco to the Sandwich Islands. . . . For forty-eight hours no table could be set, and every body had to eat as best they might under the circumstances. Most of the party went hungry, though, and attended to their praying. But there was one set of "seven-up" players who nailed a card-table to the floor and stuck to their game through thick and thin. Captain F——, of a great banking-house in San Francisco, a man of great coolness and presence of mind, was of this party.

One night the storm suddenly culminated in a climax of unparalleled fury; the vessel went down on her beam ends, and every thing let go with a crash—passengers, tables, cards, bottles—every thing came clattering to the floor in a chaos of disorder and confusion. In a moment fifty sore distressed and pleading voices ejaculated, "O Heaven! help us in our extremity!" and one voice rang out clear and sharp above the plaintive chorus and said, "Remember, boys, I played the tray for low!"

"Remarkable Instances of Presence of Mind," *Celebrated Jumping Frog of Calaveras County, and Other Sketches* (1867), 172–73.

22. Twenty or thirty years ago, when missionary enterprise was in its infancy among the islands of the South Seas, Captain Summers anchored his sloop-of-war off one of the Marquesas, I think it was. The next morning he saw an American flag floating from the beach, union down. This excited him fearfully, of course, and he sent off a boat at once to inquire into the matter. Presently the boat returned, and brought a grave-looking missionary. The Captain's anxiety ran high. He said: "What's the trouble out there?—quick!"

"Well, I am grieved to say, sir," said the missionary, "that the natives have been interrupting our sacerdotal exercises."

"No!—blast their yaller hides. I'll—what—what was it you said they'd been doing?"

"It pains me, sir, to say that they have been interrupting our sacerdotal excercises."

"Interrupting your—your—h——l! Man them starboard guns! Stand by, now, to give 'em the whole battery!"

The astounded clergyman hastened to protest against such excessive rigorous measures, and finally succeeded in making the old tar understand that the natives had only been breaking up a prayer-meeting.

"Oh, devil take it, man, is that all? I thought you meant that they'd stopped your grog!"

Alta California, 4 Aug. 1867. The notebook of 15 June has the punch line obviously meant for this expurgated version: "Thought they shut off your forncation" (*N&J* 1: 336).

23.   Christ been once—never come again.

Notebook, Aug.–Oct. 1867 (*N&J* 1: 449). An Abe Lincoln story tells of Jesse Dubois asking an itinerant preacher the topic of his proposed sermon. The preacher tells him, "The Second Coming of Christ." "Nonsense," roars Uncle Jesse. "If Christ had been to Springfield once, and got away, he'd be damned clear of coming again" (*AL Laughing,* 26). MT used it in a letter to the *Alta,* 5 Apr. 1868, from Jerusalem, asserting that the second coming would have taken place elsewhere.

24.   Sylla & Carybdis.

Notebook, Aug.–Oct. 1867 (*N&J* 1: 449). This is a hint for the incident in *Innocents Abroad* (1869), 338–39. The Oracle surprises his shipmates by coming on deck to watch Scylla and Charybdis by moonlight. He says, "I wish to see *all* the places that's mentioned in the Bible." Informed that this place is not mentioned in the Bible, he demands to know what place it is. "Why, it's Scylla and Charybdis." "Scylla and Cha—confound it, I thought it was Sodom and Gomorrah!"

25.   Whisky taken into Com[mittee] rooms in demijohns & carried out in demagogues.

Notebook, Aug.–Dec. 1867 (*N&J* 1: 488) among notes kept during his brief tour as secretary to Sen. William M. Stewart of Nevada. MT lived in Washington, D.C., Nov. 1867–Mar. 1868.

1868

26. Two indians at dinner with whites—one ate spoonful mustard—other said "What crying about?"

"Thinking about the good old Chief that died."

No. 2 took mustard—"What *you* crying about?"

"Thinking what a pity you didn't die when the old Chief did!"

Notebook, July 1868 (*N&J* 1: 516). This perennial favorite in the jestbooks was entry 235 in *Joe Miller's Jests* (1739).

27. Political parties who accuse the one in power of gobbling the spoils &c, are like the wolf who looked in at the door & saw the shepherds eating mutton & said—

"Oh certainly—it's all right as long as it's *you*—but there'd be hell to pay if I was to do that!"

Notebook, July 1868 (*N&J* 1: 516). In Fable 201 of Thomas Jones, *Aesop's Fables* (1848), 215, the wolf's last line is: "A pretty row would these men have made if they had caught me at such a supper."

1869

28. [Celebrating the patience of A.W. Olliver, a newcomer remarkable for doing as Nevadans did without complaining:] We built a Humboldt house. It is done this way. You dig a square in the steep base of the mountain, and set up two uprights and top them with two joists. Then you stretch a great sheet of "cotton domestic" from the point where the joists join the hill-side down over the joists to the ground; this makes the roof and the front of the mansion; the sides and back are the dirt walls your digging has left. A chimney is easily made by turning up one corner of the roof.

Oliver was sitting alone in this dismal den, one night, by a sage-brush fire, writing poetry; he was very fond of digging poetry out of himself—or blasting it out when it came hard. He heard an animal's footsteps close to the roof; a stone or two and some dirt came through and fell by him. He grew uneasy and said "Hi!—clear out from there, can't you!"—from time to time. But by and by he fell asleep where he sat, and pretty soon a mule fell down the chimney! The fire flew in every direction, and Oliver went over backwards.

About ten nights after that, he recovered confidence enough to go to writing poetry again. Again he dozed off to sleep, and again a mule fell down the chimney. This time, about half of that side of the house came in with the mule. Struggling to get up, the mule kicked the candle out and smashed most of the kitchen furniture, and raised considerable dust. These violent awakenings must have been annoying to Oliver, but he never complained. He moved to a mansion on the opposite side of the cañon, because he had noticed the mules did not go there.

One night about eight o'clock he was endeavoring to finish his poem, when a stone rolled in—then a hoof appeared below the canvas—then part of a cow—the after part. He leaned back in dread, and shouted "Hooy! hooy! get out of this!" and the cow struggled manfully—lost ground steadily—dirt and dust streamed down, and before Oliver could get well away, the entire cow crashed through on to the table and made a shapeless wreck of every thing!

Then, for the first time in his life, I think, Oliver complained. He said, *"This thing is growing monotonous!"*

The Innocents Abroad (1869), 286–87. Olliver served as probate judge, Humboldt County, Dec. 1861–Sept. 1863.

29.   [After learning how expensive it would be to sail the Sea of Galilee, the group abandons the excursion:] Oh, shameful, shameful ending, after such unseemly boasting! It was too much like "Ho! let me at him!" followed by a prudent "Two of you hold him—one can hold me!"

Ibid., 497–98. The allusion is to a well-worn joke, current in *Harper's Monthly* 29 (Nov. 1864): 820: A lawyer and farmer fight until the lawyer cries, "Hold us, boys! hold us! Two of you hold him; one can hold me!" *Harper's* calls it "a California story."

The next half-dozen entries are from the column "People and Things" in the Buffalo *Express,* Aug.– Sept. 1869, reprinted in Merle Johnson, *A Bibliography of MT* (1935), 178–86.

30. Every newspaper that comes to hand here lately mentions that Mr. John Holland, of Bristol, R.I., is 102 years old, and never drank a glass of liquor in his life. There is nothing so wonderful about that. We have known men not half as old who could say the same thing.

Aug. 18.

31. The king of Italy has added three dollars and a half a year to the pay of his soldiers. They only got seven dollars a year before this. But will they really be any happier now than they were when they were poor?

Aug. 21.

32. Mr. Eddes, an octogenarian, residing in Dover, Me., never saw but two steamboats—Fulton's original and a small one on Sebec Lake. He has not been in Bangor, his nearest city, in thirty-eight years. His mind is said to be richly stored with lack of information.

Aug. 23.

33. Peach kernels contain hydrocyanic (or prussic) acid, and are dangerous nutriment. Fifteen hundred of them taken on an empty stomach will kill a man.

Aug. 24.

34. John Wagner, the oldest man in Buffalo—104 years— recently walked a mile and a half in two weeks. He is as cheerful and bright as any of these other old men that charge around so in the newspapers, and is in every way as remarkable. Last November he walked five blocks in a rainstorm without any shelter but an umbrella, and cast his vote for Grant, remarking that he had voted for forty-seven presidents—which was a lie. His "second crop of rich brown hair" arrived from New York yesterday, and he has a new set of teeth coming—from Philadelphia. He is to be married next week to a girl 102 years old, who still takes in washing. They have been engaged 89 years, but their parents persistently refused their consent until three days ago. John Wagner is two years older than the Rhode Island veteran, and yet has never tasted a drop of liquor in his life, unless you count whisky.

Aug. 25.

35. [Commemorating W. Frank Stewart, San Jose, California, saloon keeper who invented a machine for determining the direction of earthquake shocks:] It was simply a lead pencil fastened in such a manner with its point against a sheet of white paper that it would make a mark up and down, across or zigzag, when the house was shaken by an earthquake; and so, whenever Stewart was shaken out of his boots or his bed, he did not rush for the streets, as other citizens did, but rushed to see what the earthquake had written him as to what direction it was traveling and whither it was probably bound. The building was a small frame one, and the hogs got to scraping themselves against it for comfort; their performances were faithfully recorded by the earthquake machine, and as faithfully reported to the public by Stewart, until he found out the fraud at last—and none too soon for his reputation as an earthquake expert.

Sept. 10.

1870

36. It is said that once a man of small consequence died, and the Rev. T.K. Beecher was asked to preach the funeral sermon—a man who abhors the lauding of people, either dead or alive, except in dignified and simple language, and then only for merits which they actually possessed or possess, not merits which they merely ought to have possessed. The friends of the deceased got up a stately funeral. They must have had misgivings that the corpse might not be praised strongly enough, for they prepared some manuscript headings and notes in which nothing was left unsaid on that subject that a fervid imagination and an unabridged dictionary could compile, and these they handed to the minister as he entered the pulpit. They were merely intended as suggestions, and so the friends were filled with consternation when the minister stood up in the pulpit and proceeded to read off the curious odds and ends in ghastly detail and in a loud voice! And their consternation solidified to petrifaction when he paused at the end, contemplated the multitude reflectively, and then said, impressively: "The man would be a fool who tried to add anything to that. Let us pray!"

"Post-mortem Poetry," *The $30,000 Bequest and Other Stories* (1906), 251–52. The story is dated: "Written in 1870."

1870–1871

The next seven entries are from the column "Memoranda," *The Galaxy*, May 1870–Apr. 1871.

37. The aged Professor [Benjamin, Sr.] Silliman took the homely-looking specimen of New Jersey coal, and said he would make a test and determine its quality. The next day the owners of the grand discovery waited on him again, eager to hear the verdict which was to make or mar their fortunes. The Professor said, with that impressive solemnity which always marked his manner:

"Gentlemen, I understand you to say that this property is situated upon a hill-top — consequently the situation is prominent. It is valuable — immensely valuable — though as a coal mine I am obliged to observe that it is a failure. Fence it in, gentlemen — fence it in, and hold to it through good and evil fortune till the Last Day; for I am convinced that it will be the best point from which to view the sublime spectacle of the final conflagration. I feel satisfied that if any part of the earth shall remain uninjured after that awful fire, it will be this coal mine of yours!"

9 (May 1870): 726.

38. There are some natures which never grow large enough to speak out and say a bad act *is* a bad act, until they have inquired into the politics or the nationality of the man who did it. And they are not really scarce, either. Cain is branded a murderer so heartily and unanimously in America, only because he was neither a Democrat nor a Republican. The Feejee Islander's abuse of Cain ceased very suddenly when the white man mentioned casually that Cain was a Feejee Islander. The next remark of the savage, after an awkward pause, was: "Well, what did Abel come fooling around there for?"

Ibid.

39.   When the lamented Judge Bagley tripped and fell down the court-house stairs and broke his neck, it was a great question how to break the news to poor Mrs. Bagley. But finally the body was put into Higgins's wagon and he was instructed to take it to Mrs. B., but to be very guarded and discreet in his language, and not break the news to her at once, but do it gradually and gently. When Higgins got there with his sad freight, he shouted till Mrs. Bagley came to the door. Then he said:
   "Does the widder Bagley live here?"
   "The *widow* Bagley? *No, Sir!*"
   "I'll bet she does. But have it your own way. Well, does *Judge* Bagley live here?"
   "Yes, Judge Bagley lives here."
   "I'll bet he don't. But never mind—it ain't for me to contradict. Is the Judge in?"
   "No, not at present."
   "I jest expected as much. Because, you know—take hold o' suthin', mum, for I'm a-going to make a little communication, and I reckon maybe it'll jar you some. There's been an accident, mum. I've got the old Judge curled up out here in the wagon— and when you see him you'll acknowledge, yourself, that an inquest is about the only thing that could be a comfort to *him!*"

9 (June 1870): 862. A later version of this event unconnected with MT is given in Mody C. Boatright, *Folk Laughter on the American Frontier* (1949), 19, where it concludes with the widow's saying, "I am not a widow" and the carter replying, "I'll bet you ten dollars you are."

40.   From Missouri a friend furnishes the following information upon a matter which has probably suggested an inquiry in more than one man's mind: "A venerable and greatly esteemed and respected old patriarch, late of this vicinity, divulged to me, on his death-bed, the origin of a certain popular phrase or figure of speech. He said it came about in this wise: A gentleman was blown up on a Mississippi steamboat, and he went up in the air about four or four and a half miles, and then, just before parting into a great variety of fragments, he remarked to a neighbor who was sailing past on a lower level, 'Say, friend, how is this for high?'"

10 (Oct. 1870): 576.

41. [At breakfast the landlady laments the death of a neighbor's servant:] "Ah, to think of it, only to think of it!—the poor old faithful creature. For she was *so* faithful. Would you believe it, she had been a servant in that self-same house and that self-same family for twenty-seven years come Christmas, and never a cross word and never a lick! And oh to think she should meet such a death at last!—a-sitting over the red-hot stove at three o'clock in the morning and went to sleep and fell on it and was actually *roasted*! not just frizzled up a bit, but literally roasted to a crisp! Poor faithful creature, how she *was* cooked! I am but a poor woman, but even if I have to scrimp to do it, I will put up a tombstone over that lone sufferer's grave—and Mr. Riley, if you would have the goodness to think up a little epitaph to put on it which would sort of describe the awful way in which she met her—"

"Put it '*Well done*, good and faithful servant!'" said Riley, and never smiled.

10 (Nov. 1870): 727. A note adds: "I have either printed that anecdote once before or told it in company so many thousand times as to carry that seeming to my mind, but it is of no consequence—it is worth printing half a dozen times." He had printed a truncated version in the Chicago *Republican* in Apr. 1868 and in the Buffalo *Express*, 29 Oct. 1870. A month after that, his friend the San Francisco–Washington correspondent J.H. Riley sailed for South Africa where he would die from blood poisoning.

1871

42. While up the river I heard the following story, showing how an animal can rise when necessary superior to its nature:

"You see," said the narrator, "the beaver took to the water and the dog was after him. First the beaver was ahead and then the dog. It was tuck and nip whether the dog would catch the beaver, and nuck and tip whether the beaver would catch the dog. Finally the beaver got across the river and the dog had almost caught him, when, phit! up the beaver skun up a tree."

"But," said a bystander, "beavers can't climb trees."

"A beaver can't climb a tree? By gosh, he *had* to climb a tree, the dog was a crowdin him so!"

11 (Jan. 1871): 156.

43.   John James Godfrey was the son of poor but honest parents in the State of Mississippi—boyhood friend of mine—bosom comrade in later years. Heaven rest his noble spirit, he is gone from us now. John James Godfrey was hired by the Hayblossom Mining Company in California to do some blasting for them—the "Incorporated Company of Mean Men," the boys used to call it. Well, one day he drilled a hole about four feet deep and put in an awful blast of powder, and was standing over it ramming it down with an iron crowbar about nine foot long, when the cussed thing struck a spark and fired the powder, and scat! away John Godfrey whizzed like a sky-rocket, him and his crowbar! Well, sir, he kept on going up in the air higher and higher, till he didn't look any bigger than a boy—and he kept going on up higher and higher, till he didn't look any bigger than a doll—and he kept on going up higher and higher, till he didn't look any bigger than a little small bee—and then he went out of sight! Presently he came in sight again, looking like a little small bee—and he came along down further and further, till he looked as big as a doll again—and down further and further, till he was as big as a boy again—and further and further, till he was a full-sized man once more; and him and his crowbar came a wh-izzing down and lit right exactly in the same old tracks and went to r-ramming down, and r-ramming down, and r-ramming down again, just the same as if nothing had happened! Now don't you know that poor cuss warn't gone only sixteen minutes, and yet that Incorporated Company of Mean Men DOCKED HIM FOR THE LOST TIME!"

11 (Apr. 1871): 617. Better known as part of ch. 36, vol. 2 of *Rough-*

ing It, this was used as early as 1867 when, according to his niece, MT used it in an address to a St. Louis Sunday school class; S.C. Webster, *MT Business Man* (1946), 92. In 1898 Joel Benton recalled a version with the pay being docked for five minutes rather than sixteen; *Harper's Monthly* 96 (Mar. 1898): 610.

1872

The next five entries are from *Roughing It,* published Feb. 1872.

44. [Describing the meal at the stage station:] We could not eat the bread or the meat, nor drink the "slumgullion." And when I looked at that melancholy vinegar-cruet, I thought of the anecdote (a very, very old one, even at that day) of the traveler who sat down to a table which had nothing on it but a mackerel and a pot of mustard. He asked the landlord if this was all. The landlord said:

"*All!* Why, thunder and lightning, I should think there was mackerel enough there for six."

"But I don't like mackerel."

"Oh—then help yourself to the mustard."

P. 44. In George Derby, *Phoenixiana* (1856), 211, the scene is an army outpost in New Mexico where the meal is "a large tin pan full of boiled rice, and a broken bottle half full of mustard."

45. [Mention of legendary stage-driver Ben Holliday excuses the insertion of a dialogue (from "my Holy Land note-book") between nineteen-year-old New Yorker Jack and the tour's pedant, who chides him for asking "Moses *who?*"] "Moses *who!* Jack, you ought to be ashamed of yourself—you ought to be ashamed of such criminal ignorance. Why, Moses, the great guide, soldier, poet, lawgiver of ancient Israel! Jack, from this spot where we stand, to Egypt, stretches a fearful desert three hundred miles in extent—and across that desert that wonderful man brought the children of Israel!—guiding them with unfailing sagacity for forty years over the sandy desolation and among the obstructing rocks and hills, and landed them at last, safe and sound, within sight of this very spot; and where we now stand they entered the

Promised Land with anthems of rejoicing! It was a wonderful, wonderful thing to do, Jack! Think of it!"

"*Forty years? Only three hundred miles?* Humph! Ben Holliday would have fetched them through in thirty-six hours!"

Pp. 58–59.

46. A young half-breed with a complexion like a yellow-jacket asked me if I would have my boots blacked. It was at the Salt Lake House the morning after we arrived. I said yes, and he blacked them. Then I handed him a silver five-cent piece, with the benevolent air of a person who is conferring wealth and blessedness upon poverty and suffering. The yellow-jacket took it with what I judged to be suppressed emotion, and laid it reverently down in the middle of his broad hand. Then he began to contemplate it, much as a philosopher contemplates a gnat's ear in the ample field of his microscope. Several mountaineers, teamsters, stage-drivers, etc. drew near and dropped into the tableau and fell to surveying the money with that attractive indifference to formality which is noticeable in the hardy pioneer. Presently the yellow-jacket handed the half dime back to me and told me I ought to keep my money in my pocket-book instead of in my soul, and then I wouldn't get it cramped and shriveled up so!

Pp. 138–39.

47. [In the course of Jim Blaine's story of the old ram:] Parson Hagar belonged to the Western Reserve Hagars; prime family; his mother was a Watson; one of his sisters married a Wheeler; they settled in Morgan county, and he got nipped by the machinery in a carpet factory and went through in less than a quarter of a minute; his widder bought the piece of carpet that had his remains wove in, and people come a hundred mile to 'tend the funeral. There was fourteen yards in the piece. She wouldn't let them roll him up, but planted him just so—full length. The church was middling small where they preached the funeral, and they had to let one end of the coffin stick out the window. They didn't bury him—they planted one end, and let him stand up, same as a monument. And they nailed a sign on it and put—put on—put on it—[the narrator is dropping off to sleep] sacred to—the m-e-m-o-r-y—of fourteen y-a-r-d-s—of three-ply—car - - - pet containing all that was—m-o-r-t-a-l—of—of—W-i-l-l-i-a-m—W-h-e—"

P. 389. The simplest summary of Jim Blaine's story of his grandfather's ram is in MT's New York speech, 19 Apr. 1906 (Fatout, 516–17):

I'm going along like an old man I used to know, who used to start to tell a story about his grandfather. He had an awfully retentive memory, and he never finished the story, because he switched off into something else. He used to tell about how his grandfather one day went into a pasture, where there was a ram. The old man dropped a silver dime in the grass, and stooped over to pick it up. The ram was observing him, and took the old man's action as an invitation.

Just as he was going to finish about the ram this friend of mine would recall that his grandfather had a niece who had a glass eye. She used to loan that glass eye to another lady friend, who used it when she received company. The eye didn't fit the friend's face, and it was loose. And whenever she winked it would turn over.

Then he got on the subject of accidents, and he would tell a story about how he believed accidents never happened.

"There was an Irishman coming down a ladder with a hod of bricks," he said, "and a Dutchman was standing on the ground below. The Irishman fell on the Dutchman and killed him. Accident? Never! If the Dutchman hadn't been there the Irishman would have been killed. Why didn't the Irishman fall on a dog which was next to the Dutchman? Because the dog would have seen him coming."

Then he'd get off from the Dutchman to an uncle named Reginald Wilson. Reginald went into a carpet factory one day, and got twisted into the machinery's belt. . . . And so on he would ramble about telling the story of his grandfather until we never were told whether he found the ten-cent piece or whether something else happened.

48.   Fort Yuma is probably the hottest place on earth. The thermometer stays at one hundred and twenty in the shade there all the time—except when it varies and goes higher. It is a U.S. military post, and its occupants get so used to the terrific heat that they suffer without it. There is a tradition (attributed to John Phenix [It has been purloined by fifty different scribblers who were too poor to invent a fancy but not ashamed to steal one.—M.T.]) that a very, very wicked soldier died there, once, and of course, went straight to the hottest corner of perdition,—and the next day he *telegraphed back for his blankets.*

P. 412. George Derby's biographer, G.R. Stewart, assumes that MT's aside in brackets alludes to J. Ross Browne's lifting this anecdote from Derby for his own *Adventures in the Apache Country* (1868); *John Phoenix Esq.* (1937), 224.

1873

49.   In America—man murdered his father and mother—and [plea] is being orphan.

Dictation, 10 June 1873; *N&J* 1: 527. Artemus Ward, "A Hard Case," *Works* (1879), 100, tells about a fourteen-year-old Arkansas lad who kills both his parents and pleads for mercy as an orphan; Lincoln also used the general idea (*AL Laughing*, 91).

1876

50.   In church last Sunday I listened to a charity sermon. My first impulse was to give three hundred and fifty dollars: I repented of that and reduced it a hundred; repented of that and reduced it another hundred; repented of that and reduced the remaining fifty to twenty-five; repented of that and dropped to two dollars and a half; when the plate came around at last, I repented once more and contributed ten cents. Well, when I got home, I did wish to goodness I had that ten cents back again!

"The Facts Concerning the Recent Carnival of Crime in Connecticut," *Atlantic Monthly* 37 (June 1876): 647. For variant, see **287**.

The next seven entries are the entire text of a pamphlet circulating in private editions numbering upwards of fifty since its first printing—four copies—in 1880. Variously titled "Date 1601" and "Conversation, as it was by the Social Fireside in the Time of the Tudors," MT wrote it in 1876 while polishing *Tom Sawyer* and beginning *Huckleberry Finn.* He said it was intended to acquaint his friend the Rev. Joseph Twichell with the language and customs in the time of Queen Elizabeth, adding, "I can hardly think of that thing without laughing"; *MT's Note-*

book, ed. Paine, 151. In 1882 MT himself sent a manuscript to Lt. C.E.S.
Wood at West Point, where an edition of fifty copies was printed off.
That edition is the source of the present reprinting, which departs from
the original, however, in modernizing the long "s" and long "f" and
reducing the superscriptions for "ye, Wch," and the like. Otherwise, the
visual chaos remains as a vital part of the general burlesque. Modern
readers should have little trouble decoding the system, however incon-
sistent: "an" usually means "if"; "ye," "ys" and "yt" signify "the," "this,"
and "that"; the tilde above a vowel signifies a nasal—"thē" could mean
"then" or "them" depending on context. The authoritative scholarly study
of the text is by F. J. Meine for the MT Society of Chicago (1939).

51. *Date 1601.* Conversation, as it was by the Social Fireside,
in the Time of the Tudors. [Mem.—The following is supposed to
be an extract from the diary of the Pepys of that day, the same
being cup-bearer to Queen Elizabeth. It is supposed that he is
of ancient and noble lineage; that he despises these literary *ca-
naille*; that his soul consumes with wrath to see the Queen stoop-
ing to talk with such; and that the old man feels his nobility de-
filed by contact with Shakespere, etc., and yet he has *got* to stay
there till Her Majesty chooses to dismiss him.]

Yesternight toke her maiestie ye queene a fantasie such as shee
sometimes hath, & hadde to her closet certaine yt doe write playes,
bookes, & svch like, these beeing my lord Bacon, his worship Sr.
Walter Ralegh, Mr. Ben Jonson, & ye childe Francis Beaumonte,
wch beeing but sixteen, hath yet turned his hād to ye doing of
ye Lattin masters into our Englyche tong, with grete discretion
& much applaus. Also came with these ye famous Shaxpur. A
righte straunge mixing truly of mighty bloud with meā, ye more
in especial syns ye queenes grace was present, as likewyse these
following, *to wit*: Ye Duchesse of Bilgewater, twenty-two yeeres
of age; ye Countesse of Granby, twenty-six; her doter, ye Lady
Helen, fifteen; as also these two maides of honor, *to wit*: ye Lady
Margery Boothy, sixty-five, & ye Lady Alice Dilberry, turned
seuenty, shee beeing two yeeres ye queenes graces elder.

I beeing her maisty's cup-bearer, hadde no choyce but to re-
mayne & behold ranke forgotte, & ye high holde conuerse wh
ye low as uppon equal termes, a grete scandal did ye world heare
therof.

52.   In ye heat of ye talke it befel yt one did breake wind, yield-
ing an exceding mighty & distressfull stink, whereat all did laffe
full sore, and thē:

Ye Queene. Verily in mine eight and sixty yeeres have I not
heard ye fellow to this fart. Meseemeth, by ye grete sound and
clamour of it, it was male; yet ye belly it did lurk behinde shoulde
now fall lene & flat agaynst ye spine of him yt hath beene delivered of so stately & so vaste a bulke, whereas ye guts of them
yt doe quiff-splitters bear, stand comely still & rounde. Prithee,
lette ye author confesse ye offspring. Wil my Lady Alice testify?

Lady Alice. Good your grace, an' I hadde room for such a
thundergust within mine auncient bowels, 'tis not in reason I could
discharge ye same & live to thanck God for yt Hee did chuse
handmayd so humble whereby to shew his power. Nay, 'tis not
I yt have broughte forth ys ryche o'ermastering fog, ys fragrant
gloom, so pray you seeke ye further.

Ye Queene. Mayhap ye Lady Margery hath done ye companie
this favour?

Lady Margerey. So please you madā, my limbs are feeble wh
ye weighte and drouth of fiue & sixty winters, & it behoveth yt
I be tender vnto thē. In ye good providence of God, an' *I* hadde
contained ys wonder, forsoothe wolde I haue gi'en ye whole eue-
ning of my sinking life to ye dribbling of it forth, wh trembling
& vneasy sould, not launched it suddē in its matchlesse might,
taking myne owne life with uiolence, rending my weak frame like
rottē rags. It was not I, your maisty.

Ye Queene. O' God's naym, who hath favoured us? Hath it
come to pass yt a fart shall fart *itselfe?* Not soche a one as this,
I trow. Young Master Beaumont; but no, 'twould have wafted him
to Heav'n like down of goose's boddy. 'Twas not ye little Lady
Helen—nay, ne'er blush, my child; thou'lt tickle thy tender maidēhedde with many a mousie-squeak before thou learnest to blow
a harricane like this. Was't you, my learned & ingenious Jonson?

Jonson. So fell a blast hath ne'er mine ears saluted, nor yet
a stench so all-pervading & immortal. 'Twas not a nouice did it,
good your maiestie, but one of ueterā experiēce—else hadde hee
fayled of confidence. In sooth it was not I.

Ye Queene. My lord Bacon?

Lord Bacon. Not from my leãe ẽtrailes hath this prodigie burst forth, so please your grace. Nau't doth so befit ye grete as grete performance; & haply shall ye finde yt 'tis not from mediocrity this miracle hath issued.

(Tho' ye subject bee but a fart, yet will ys tedious sink of learning ponderously philosophize. Meantime did ye foul & deadly stink peruade all places to yt degree, yt never smelt I ye like, yet dared I not to leave ye presẽce, albeit I was like to suffocate.)

Ye Queene. What saith ye worshipful Master Shaxpur?

Shaxpur. In ye grete hãd of God I stand, & so proclaim my innocence. Tho'gh ye sinless hosts of Heav'n hadde foretold ye comyng of ys most desolating breath, proclaiming it a werke of uninspired mã, its quaking thunders, its firmamẽt-clogging rottennesse his own achievemẽt in due course of nature, yet hadde not I believed it; but hadde sayd ye pit itself hath furnished forth ye stink, & Heav'n's artillery hath shook ye globe in admiration of it.

(Thẽ was there a silence, & each did turne him toward ye worshipful Sr Walter Ralegh, yt brown'd, embatteld, bloudy swashbuckler, who rising vp did smile, & simpering, say:)

Sr W. Most gracious maiestie, 'twas I yt did it, but indeed it was so poor & frail a note, compared with such as I ã wont to furnish, yt in sooth I was ashamed to call ye weakling mine in soe august a presẽce. It was nothing—less thã nothing, madam, I did it but to clere my nether throat; but hadde I come prepared thẽ hadde I delivered something worthy. Bear with mee, please your grace, till I can make amends.

(Thẽ delivered hee himselfe of such a godlesse & rock-shivering blast yt all were fain to stop their ears, & following it did come so dense & foul a stink yt that which went before did seeme a poor & trifling thing beside it. Thẽ saith he, feigning yt he blushed & was confused, *I perceive that I am weak to-daie & cannot justice doe unto my powers*; & sat him down as who sholde say, *There it is not moche; yet he that hath an arse to spare lette hym fellow that, an' hee think hee can.* By God, an' I were ye queene, I wolde e'en tip ys swaggering braggart out o' the court, & lette him air his grandeurs & break his intolerable wynd before ye deaf & such as suffocation pleseth.)

53. The fell they to talke about ye manners & cust'ms of many peoples, & Master Shaxpur spake of ye booke of ye sieur Michael de Montaine, wherein was mention of ye coustom of widows of Perigord to wear vppon ye hedde-dress, in sign of widowhood, a jewel in ye similitude of a man's mēber wilted & limber, whereat ye queene did laffe & say, widows in England doe wear prickes too, but 'twixt ye thyghs, & not wilted neither, till coition hath done that office for thē. Master Shaxpur did likewise observe how yt ye sieur de Montaine hath also spoken of a certaine emperour of soche mightie prowesse yt hee did take ten maidē-heddes in ye compass of a single night, ye while his empresse did entertain two & twēty lusty knights atweene her sheetes, yet was not satisfide; whereat ye merrie Countesse Granby saith a ram is yet ye emperour's superiour, sith hee wil tup above an hundred yewes 'twixt sunne & sunne, & after, if yt hee can have none more to shag, wil masturbate until hee hath enrych'd whole acres wh hys seed.

The spake ye damned wyndmill, Sr Walter, of a people in ye vttermost parts of America yt copulate not vntil they be fiue-&-thirty yeers of age, ye womē heeing eight-&-twenty, & doe it thē but once in sevē yeeres.

Ye Queene. How doth thatte like my lyttle Lady Helen? Shall we send thee thither & preserve thy belly?

Lady Helen. Please yr highnesses grace, mine old nurse hath told mee there bee more ways of seruing God thā by locking ye thyghs together; yet ā I willing to serue him yt way too, sith yovr highnesses grace hath set ye ensample.

Ye Queene. God's wowndes a good ansvver, childe.

Lady Alice. Mayhap 'twill weakē whē ye hair sprouts below ye navel.

Lady Helen. Nay, it sprouted two yeeres syne; I can scarce more thā cover it with my hād now.

Ye Queene. Hear ye thatte, my little Beaumonte? Have ye not a smalle birde about ye that stirs at hearing tel of soe sweete a neste?

Beaumonte. 'Tis not insēsible, illustrious madā; but mousing owls & bats of low degree may not aspire to bliss soe whelming & ecstatic as is found in ye downie nests of birdes of Paradise.

Ye Queene. By ye gullet of God, 'tis a neat-turned complimēt. With soche a tong as thyne, lad, thou'lt spread the ivorie thyghs of many a willing mayd in thy good time, an' thy cod-piece bee as handy as thy speeche.

Then spake ye queene of how shee met old Rabelais whē shee was turned of fifteen, & hee did tel her of a man his father knew that hadde a double pair of bollocks, whereon a controversy followed as concerning the most just way to spell ye word, ye contention running high 'twixt ye learned Bacon & ye ingenious Jonson, until at last ye old Lady Margery, wearying of it all, saith, "Gentles, what mattereth it how ye shal spell ye word? I warrāt ye whē ye use yr bollocks ye shall not think of it; & my Lady Granby, bee ye content; lette ye spelling bee; you shal enjoy ye beating of them on your buttocks just ye same, I trow. Before I hadde gained my fourteenth yeere I hadde learnt yt them yt would explore a cunt stop'd not to consider the spelling o't."

Sr W. In sooth, whē a shift's turned upp delay is meet for naught but dalliance. Boccaccio hath a story of a priest yt did beguile a mayd into his cell, thē knelt him in a corner for to pray for grace yt hee bee rightly thanckfvll for ys tēder maidēhedde ye Lord hadde sent him; but ye abbot spying through ye key-hole, did see a tuft of brownish hair with fair white flesh about it, wherefore whē ye priest's prayer was donne, his chance was gone, forasmuch as ye lyttle mayde hadde but ye one cunt, & yt was already occupied to her content.

54. Thē conversed they of religion, & ye mightie werke ye olde dead Luther did doe by ye grace of God. Thē next about poetry, & Master Shaxpur did rede a parte of his Kyng Henry iv, ye which, it seemeth vnto mee, is not of ye ualve of an arsefvl of ashes, yet they praised it bravely, one & all.

Ye same did rede a portion of his "Venvs & Adonis," to their prodigious admiration, vvhereas I, beeing sleepy & fatigved withal, did deme it but paltrie stoffe, & was the more discomforted in yt ye bloudie bucanier hadde gotte his wynd again, & did turne his mind to farting with such uillain zeal yt presently I was like to choke once more. God damn this wyndy ruffian & all his breed. I wolde yt hell mighte gette hym.

55. They talked about ye wonderful defense which olde Sr
Nickolas Throgmorton did make for himselfe before ye judges
in ye time of Mary; wch was unlvcky matter for to broach, sith
it fetched out ye queene with a *Pity yt hee, hauing soe moche
wit, hadde yet not enough to save his doter's maiden hedde sounde
for her marriage-bedde.* And ye queene did give ye damn'd Sr.
Walter a look yt made hym wince—for shee hath not forgot hee
was her own lover in yt olde daie. There was silent uncomfortable-
ness now; 'twas not a good turne for talk to take, sith if ye queene
must find offense in a little harmlesse debauching, when pricks
were stiff & cunts not loath to take ye stiffness out of them, who
of ys companie was sinless; beholde was not ye wife of Master Shaxpur four months gone with child whē she stood uppe before ye
altar? Was not her Grace of Bilgewater roger'd by four lords before she hadde a husband? Was not ye lyttle Lady Helen born
on her mother's wedding-day? And, beholde, were not ye Lady
Alice & ye Lady Margery there, mouthing religion, whores from
ye cradle?

Throckmorton, who died in 1571 when daughter Bess was only five,
gained acquittal of treason; Queen Mary imprisoned the jury that ac-
quitted him. Twenty years later Raleigh had to marry Bess when he got
her with child.

56. In time came they to discourse of Ceruātes, & of ye new
painter, Rubēs, yt is begynning to bee heard of. Fine words &
dainty-wrought phrases from ye ladies now, one or two of them
beeing, in other days pupils of yt poor ass, Lille [John Lyly], himself; & I marked how yt Jonson & Shaxpur did fidget to discharge
some uenom of sarcasm, yet dared they not in ye presence, ye
queene's grace beeing ye uery flower of ye Euphuists herselfe. But
behold, there bee they yt, having a specialtie, & admiring it in
themselues, bee jealous when a neighbour doth essaye it, nor can
bide it in them long. Wherefore 'twas observable yt ye queene
waxed uncontent; & in tyme a labor'd grandiose speech out of
ye mouthe of Lady Alice, who manifestly did mightily pride herself thereon, did quite exhavste ye queene's endurance, who listened till ye gaudy speeche was done, thē lifted up her brows,

& with uaste irony, mincing sayth, "Oshit!" Whereat they all did
laffe, but not ye Lady Alice, yt olde foolish bitche.

57.   Now was Sr Walter minded of a tale hee once did hear ye
ingenious Margarette of Navarre relate, about a maid, which beeing like to suffer rape by an olde archbishoppe, did smartly con-
triue a deuice to saue her maydēhedde, & said to him, "First,
my lord, I prithee, take out thy holy tool & piss before mee," wch
doing, lo hys member felle, & wolde not rise again.

1877

58.   Among other talk, today, it came out that whale-ships carry
no doctor. The captain adds the doctorship to his own duties.
He not only gives medicines, but sets broken limbs after notions
of his own, or saws them off and sears the stump when amputa-
tion seems best. The captain is provided with a medicine-chest,
with the medicines numbered instead of named. A book of directions goes with this. It describes diseases and symptoms, and says,
"Give a teaspoonful of No. 9 once an hour," or "Give ten grains
of No. 12 every half hour," etc. One of our sea-captains came across
a skipper in the North Pacific who was in a state of great surprise
and perplexity. Said he:—
    "There's something rotten about this medicine-chest business.
One of my men was sick,—nothing much the matter. I looked
in the book: it said, give him a teaspoonful of No. 15. I went
to the medicine-chest, and I see I was out of No. 15. I judged
I'd got to get up a combination somehow that would fill the bill;
so I hove into the fellow half a teaspoonful of No. 8 and half
a teaspoonful of No. 7, and I'll be hanged it it didn't kill him
in fifteen minutes! There's something about this medicine-chest
system that's too many for me!"
    "Some Rambling Notes of an Idle Excursion," *Atlantic Monthly* 40
(Nov. 1877): 588–89.

1877–1878

The next three entries are from the notebook of Nov. 1877–July 1878; *N&J* vol. 2.

59. 40 thieves—charged $1—greeny paid it but declined to enter—said he didn't care to see the other 39.

P. 54.

60. S[an] F[rancisco] man who politely measures dying man for coffin, straightens him out crosses his hands & asks him to die so.

P. 58.

61. Jim Gillis's yarn about the blue jays that tried to fill Carrington's house with acorns—[through a knothole in the roof]

"By George this lays over anything *I* ever struck," says the jay. "I've put 460 in there."

P. 65. In ch. 3 of *A Tramp Abroad* (1880) this is of course Jim Baker's tale—or half of it, since the remainder tells how flocks of jays from miles around came to solve the mystery; "Every jay in the whole lot put his eye to the hole and delivered a more chuckle-headed opinion about the mystery than the jay that went there before him. They examined the house all over, too. The door was standing half open, and at last one old jay happened to go and light on it and look in. Of course that knocked the mystery galley-west in a second." The result was a skyfull of jays guffawing "over that thing like human beings." Jays came from all over the country to see that hole, "every summer for three years. Other birds too. And they could all see the point, except an owl that come from Nova Scotia to visit the Yo Semite, and he took this thing in on his way back. He said he couldn't see anything funny in it. But then he was a good deal disappointed about Yo Semite, too" (40–42).

1878–1879

62. "I have expectorated in this beer." "Ich auch."

Notebook for Oct. 1878–Feb. 1879; *N&J* 2: 236, where the note gives

MT's translation of the story from a Mannheim newspaper: "A thirsty man called for beer. Just as the foaming mug was placed before him, some one sent in for him. The place was crowded.—Could he trust his beer there? A bright idea flashes through his brain. He writes on a card, 'I have expectorated in this beer'—fastens the card to the mug & retires with triumph in his eye to see what is wanted. He returns presently & finds his card reversed & this written on it: 'Ich auch,' (I also!)."

63.   John & Sally upstairs in back room with door locked "Don't jump to Conclusions on mere circumstantial evidence."

Ibid. 2: 280. Perhaps a garbled version of a lawyer's tale commonly attributed to Lincoln in which a farmboy rushes to his father: "Paw, come quick. The hired man and Sis are in the haymow, and he's a-pullin' down his pants and she's a-liftin' up her skirts. Paw, they're gettin' ready to pee all over our hay." "Son," said the farmer, "you've got your facts absolutely right, but you've drawn a completely wrong conclusion!" (*AL Laughing*, p. x.)

64.   I must tell you Susie's last. She is sorely badgered with dreams; & her stock dream is that she is being eaten up by bears. She is a grave & thoughtful child, as you will remember. Last night she had the usual dream. This morning she stood apart (after telling it,) for some time, looking vacantly at the floor, & absorbed in meditation. At last she looked up, & with the pathos of one who feels he has not been dealt by with even-handed fairness, said, "But mamma, the trouble is, that I am never the *bear,* but always the PERSON."

MT-Howells Letters, 1: 241–42.

1879

65.   That dear sweet old German baroness who loved to find similarities between G[erman] & E[nglish]—'Ah the 2 languages are so alike—we say Ach Gott, you say Goddam." To laugh when peop[le] are serious is not a fault of mine, but this "fetched" me.

Notebook of Feb.–Sept. 1879; *N&J* 2: 310.

66.   Joe Twichell's Decoration-day prayer—"G——d d——n that dog."

Ibid. 2: 343. In 15 Mar. 1906, MT dictated the story for his autobiography (2: 210–12): After long, hot, tedious ceremonies, tempers wore thin though the people remained attentive. Twichell began an impressive closing prayer, trying to make it brief. "In the middle of it he made a pause. The drummer thought he was through, and let fly a rub-a-dub-dub and the little major stormed out, '*Stop* that drum!' Twichell tried again. He got almost to the last word safely, when somebody trod on a dog and the dog let out a howl of anguish that could be heard beyond the frontier. The major said, "God damn that dog!"—and Twichell said, "Amen."

By coincidence perhaps, *Harper's Monthly* carried a slightly similar tale about a "Father Homer" in the issue for Dec. 1866 that carried MT's report from the Sandwich Islands, "Forty-three Days in an Open Boat" (34: 104–13). Father Homer has a whining voice. Interrupted by a whining dog, he exclaims "in his whining tone: 'O make a joyful noise unto the Lord'—put out that dog!—'Sing unto the Lord a new song'" (130).

67.   He calls it a deestrict. I can stand in the middle of it & all over it—when I'm in order.—You're out of order now. How'd *you* know it.

Ibid. 2: 344. The story is told about Arkansas state senator Cassius F. Johnson by Vance Randolph, *Pissing in the Snow* (1976), 103–104, with the concluding line: "Otherwise I could have pissed clear across the s-o-b!" Randolph notes that "a relative of MT" had a manuscript which was probably intended as a satire on early Arkansas legislators.

68.   [Allegedly an address to the Stomach Club:] My gifted predecessor has warned you against the "social evil—adultery." In his able paper he exhausted that subject; he left absolutely nothing more to be said on it. But I will continue his good work in the cause of morality by cautioning you against that species of recreation called "self-abuse" to which I perceive you are much addicted. All great writers on health and morals, both ancient and modern, have struggled with this stately subject; this shows its dignity and importance. Some of these writers have taken one side, some the other.

Homer, in the second book of the Iliad, says with fine enthusiasm, "Give me masturbation or give me death." Caesar, in his Commentaries, says, "To the lonely it is company; to the forsaken it is a friend; to the aged and to the impotent it is a benefactor. They that are penniless are yet rich, in that they still have this majestic diversion." In another place this experienced observer has said, "There are times when I prefer it to sodomy."

Robinson Crusoe says, "I cannot describe what I owe to this gentle art." Queen Elizabeth said, "It is the bulwark of Virginity." Cetewayo, the Zulu hero, remarked, "A jerk in the hand is worth two in the bush." The immortal Franklin has said, "Masturbation is the mother of invention." He also said, "Masturbation is the best policy."

Michelangelo and all the other old masters—"Old Masters," I will remark, is an abbreviation, a contraction—have used similar language. Michelangelo said to Pope Julius II, "Self-negation is noble, self-culture is beneficient, self-possession is manly, but to the truly great and inspiring soul they are poor and tame compared to self-abuse." Mr. Brown, here, in one of his latest and most graceful poems, refers to it in an eloquent line which is destined to live to the end of time—"None know it but to love it; none name it but to praise."

Such are the utterances of the most illustrious of the masters of this renowned science, and apologists for it. The name of those who decry it and oppose it, is legion; they have made strong arguments and uttered bitter speeches against it—but there is not room to repeat them here in much detail. Brigham Young, an expert of incontestable authority, said, "As compared with the other thing, it is the difference between the lightning bug and the lightning." Solomon said, "There is nothing to recommend it but its cheapness." Galen said, "It is shameful to degrade to such bestial uses that grand limb, that formidable member, which we votaries of Science dub the Major Maxillary—when they dub it at all—which is seldom. It would be better to decapitate the Major than to use him so. It would be better to amputate the os frontis than to put it to such use."

The great statistician, Smith, in his report to Parliament, says, "In my opinion, more children have been wasted in this way than in any other." It cannot be denied that the high antiquity of this art entitles it to our respect; but at the same time I think its harm-fulness demands our condemnation. Mr. Darwin was grieved to feel obliged to give up his theory that the monkey was the con-necting link between man and the lower animals. I think he was too hasty. The monkey is the only animal, except man, that prac-tices this science; hence he is our brother; there is a bond of sym-pathy and relationship between us. Give this ingenuous animal an audience of the proper kind, and he will straightway put aside his other affairs and take a whet; and you will see by his contor-tions and his ecstatic expression that he takes an intelligent and human interest in his performance.

The signs of excessive indulgence in this destructive pastime are easily detectable. They are these: A disposition to eat, to drink, to smoke, to meet together convivially, to laugh, to joke, and tell indelicate stories—and mainly, a yearning to paint pictures. The results of the habit are: Loss of memory, loss of virility, loss of cheerfulness, and loss of progeny.

Of all the various kinds of sexular intercourse, this has least to recommend it. As an amusement, it is too fleeting; as an oc-cupation, it is too wearing; as a public exhibition, there is no money in it. It is unsuited to the drawing-room, and in the most cul-tured society it has long since been banished from the social board. It has at last, in our day of progress and improvement, been de-graded to brotherhood with flatulence. Among the best bred, these two arts are now indulged in only in private—though by consent of the whole company, when only males are present, it is still permissible, in good society, to remove the embargo on the fundamental sigh.

My illustrious predecessor has taught you that all forms of the "social evil" are bad. I would teach you that some of these forms are more to be avoided than others. So, in concluding, I say, "If you *must* gamble away your lives sexually, don't play a lone hand too much." When you feel a revolutionary uprising in your sys-tem, get your Vendome Column down some other way—don't jerk it down.

Some Thoughts on the Science of Onanism, "Being an Address De-livered Before the Members of the Stomach Club, Paris, 1879" (privately printed, 1952). As Arthur Wroebel has shown in the *Journal of Popular*

Culture 15 (1982): 53–59, this was a parody of quack literature warning against masturbation. Though now reprinted in both popular (e.g., *Playboy* 21 [1974]: 157) and scholarly texts (Fatout, 125–27), it once circulated underground, sometimes in association with a poem allegedly composed for the Mammoth Cod Club:

> I thank Thee for the bull, O God,
> Whenever a steak I eat,
> The working of his mammoth cod
> Is what gives to us our meat.
>
> And for the ram, a meed of praise
> He with his mighty cod
> Foundation for our mutton lays
> With every vigorous prod.
>
> And then the boar who at his work,
> His hind hoofs fixed in sod,
> Contented packs the embryo pork
> All with his mighty cod.
>
> Of beasts, man is the only one
> Created by our God,
> Who purposely, and for mere fun,
> Plays with his mammoth cod.

A printed copy in the Huntington Library (accession no. 302375) bears an extract from MT's "letter to the Mammoth Cod Club: I wrote this little poem for the instruction of children. I wrote it to show the youth of the country that animals do better by instinct than man does by reason, unless properly guided. I intended it for Sunday schools and when sung by a hundred guileless children, it produces a very pretty effect."

1880

69. [Recalling a cartoon in a German newspaper:] I call to mind a picture of a commercial traveler who is about to unroll his samples:

Merchant. —(pettishly) No, don't. I don't want to buy anthing!
Drummer. —If you please, I was only going to show you—
Merchant. —But I don't wish to see them!

Drummer. — (after a pause, pleadingly) — But do you mind letting *me* look at them? — I haven't seen them for three weeks!

A Tramp Abroad (1880), 631.

1881

70. *Personating Mark Twain.*

We find the following in an exchange:

The Hon. DeShame Hornet had a very unpleasant experience lately. Mark Twain was advertised to lecture in the town of Glochester, but for some reason failed to get around. In the emergency the lecture committee decided to employ Mr. Hornet to deliver his celebrated address on temperance, but so late in the day was this arrangement made, that no bills announcing it could be circulated, and the audience assembled, expecting to listen to the celebrated innocent.

Nobody in the town knew Mark, or had ever heard him lecture, and they had got the notion that he was funny, and went to the lecture prepared to laugh. Even those on the platform, except the chairman, did not know Mr. Hornet from Mark Twain, and so, when he was introduced, thought nothing of the name, as they knew Mark Twain was a *nom de plume,* and supposed his real name was Hornet.

Mr. Hornet first remarked, "Intemperance is the curse of this country."

The audience burst into a merry laugh. He knew it could not be at his remark, and thought his clothes must be awry, and he asked the chairman if he was all right, and got "yes" for answer. He couldn't understand it, but went on:

"It breaks up happy homes!" — still louder mirth. "It is carrying young men down to death and hell!" — a perfect roar and applause.

Mr. Hornet began to get excited. He thought they were guying him, but he proceeded, "We must crush the serpent!" — a tremendous howl of laughter. Hornet couldn't stand it.

"What I am saying is gospel truth," he cried. The audience fairly bellowed with mirth. Hornet turned to a man on the stage, and said: "Do you see anything very ridiculous in my remarks or behavior?"

"Yes, ha ha, it's intensely funny—ha ha ha! Go on," cried the roaring man.

"This is an insult," cried Hornet, dancing wildly about. More laughter, and cries of, "Go on, Twain!"

And then the chairman got the idea of the thing, and rose up and explained the situation; and the men on the stage suddenly quit laughing, blushed very red; and the folks in the audience looked at each other in a mighty sheepish way, and they quit laughing too. And then Mr. Hornet himself became thoroughly mad, and very plainly told them he had never before got into a town so entirely populated by asses and idiots. And having said that, he left the hall.

The Californian (San Francisco) 4 (July 1881): 97–98. When Will Clemens used this anecdote in 1892 for *MT His Life and Work*, 149–51, he gave the orator's name as "Hon. Demshain Hornet" and the town as "Colchester, Connecticut."

1882–1883

71.   Man down south from New England said, "if I had heaven or home placed before me, wouldn't know which to choose"— reflected & added, "would take home—can go to heaven *any time.*"

Notebook for Jan. 1882–Feb. 1883; *N&J* 2: 488.

72.   Emerson & Artemus Ward—

Ibid. 2: 510, where the note explains the allusion: a joke about Ralph Waldo Emerson supposedly making so incoherent a public talk that the audience mistook him for Artemus Ward.

73.   A fellow was persuaded by his friends to start a hotel at a sort of Railroad junction thinking he would pick up a good business. He fitted up his place all nice—ice coolers, water-closets, &c. But his expectations not realized. People didn't patronize him much except to drink his ice water & urinate there.

One of his friends asked him how was business. He replied, "Well, I can't say exactly yet. Haven't struck a balance."

"What do you mean? Can't judge whether you are making anything?"

"Well, it stand like this:—They come here and exchange their piss for my ice water and I haven't sold the piss yet."

Notebook for Apr.–May 1882; *N&J* 2: 542.

74.   Second Mate "Dad" Dunham says he was mate on the Fannie Tatum Trip up Missouri river 3300 miles made fastest time on record viz. 3 days 9 hours and 4 months. (Capt. Ed Gray misconceived the spirit of this joke & said: "You mean 4 months 3 days and 9 hours.")

Ibid. 2: 573–74.

75.   As for me, I hope to be cremated. I made that remark to my pastor once, who said, with what he seemed to think was an impressive manner—

"I wouldn't worry about that, if I had your chances."

Life on the Mississippi (1883), 441—the page suppressed at Mrs. Clemens's request because its vignette showed MT in flames.

1884–1885

76.   Mrs. H's husband aged 92 fell & broke nose—She said it came near disfiguring him for life.

Notebook for Sept. 1884–Apr. 1885: *N&J* 3:72.

77.   The village no-'count; very sick. Minister: "You ought to call on God." "Well, I'm so kind of sick & lame I don't git out to call on anybody."

Ibid.; *N&J* 3: 74.

78.   Jim Fisk. Would his father lie? "Well, he had moral strength up to a certain strain, like the rest of us. He wouldn't tell a lie for nine pence, but he would tell 8 for a dollar."

Ibid. 3: 79. A later notebook, for May–July 1896, repeated this with a note that "9d is 12½¢."

1885

79. [Excusing his tardiness to a Burlington, Iowa, audience:] He said he had stopped through the day with his mother in Keokuk. She was eighty-two years old; she was the only mother he had; their homes being a thousand miles apart he might never see her again. He thought he could trust the St. Louis train, but his trust was betrayed. It started from Keokuk an hour late and had been getting an hour later ever since. On the way they broke something. A dispute arose as to what it was that was broken. It took forty minutes to decide the dispute, and five minutes to repair the damage.

Burlington *Hawkeye,* 16 Jan. 1885; rpt. Lorch, "MT in Iowa," 27 (1929), 529–30.

80. A number of years ago Mark Twain delivered a lecture at Mattoon, Illinois, in a public hall that had a hall above it that was used by a secret order, and during the lecture there was frequent noise from above, as if some one was being taken into the lodge with a good deal of fun, so much so that it disturbed the lecturer very much. Just before the close of the lecture Mark Twain said that he had lectured in school-houses, churches, theatres, and opera-houses, but he believed this was the first time that he had ever lectured in a livery-stable where they kept the horses overhead.

"Editor's Drawer," *Harper's Monthly* 70 (Apr. 1885): 822, probably referring to the lecture in Dec. 1871.

1885–1886

81. Bram Stoker's yarn about the Irish christening.

Notebook for Aug. 1885–Mar. 1886; *N&J* 3: 195. The story is expanded in a speech for the Savage Club, London, 29 June 1907 (Fatout, 565–66). The preacher's spread-eagled oratory concludes the christening by predicting a great career for the baby as another Napoleon or Alexander or "the greatest poet the world has ever seen; a Shakespeare, a Homer, a Shelley, a Keats, a Byron compacted into one. He may sing songs that may live as long as the land. He may become—What's his name?"—this to the father. "Mary Ann," replied the parent.

82.   [In a letter to H.W. Beecher, 11 Sept. 1885, who had asked for facts about U.S. Grant's drinking:] My idea gained from army men, is that the drunkenness (and sometimes pretty reckless spreeing, nights,) ceased before he came East to be Lt. General. . . . It was while Grant was still in the West that Mr. Lincoln said he wished he could find out what brand of whisky that fellow used, so he could furnish it to some of the other generals.

Letters, ed. Paine (1917), 2: 457–58. This was an old jestbook favorite with the King of England making the remark about General James Wolfe but it was adapted to Lincoln and Grant during the presidential campaign of 1864 and Lincoln very likely did repeat it (*AL Laughing,* 40–41).

1886–1887

83.   Procession of men hired to follow the corpse of an unpopular man at $2 apiece, & look down sorrowing; if they looked up, to be docked half. There was an evil smell. Finally they agreed that one should look & they would stand the loss between them. They found they had switched off & were following a night cart.

Notebook for Mar. 1886–June 1887; *N&J* 3: 233.

84.   Texas girl lassos wild horse & rides home; Boston girl captures codfish & rides him home astride. Burdette—"This accounts for the peculiar smell of the codfish."

Ibid. 3: 233. The joke here is that Robert J. Burdette, popular columnist and lecturer as "The Burlington Hawkeye Man," settled down as a respectable Baptist minister in Pasadena, California.

85.   Hi! mars Jesus, how's yo' pa?

Ibid. This is the conclusion of a tale often attributed to Lincoln about a balloonist "arrayed in silk and spangles" who descends in a cotton field, frightening off the slaves except for one venerable rheumatic incapable of running who greets him thus; *AL Laughing,* 136.

1887

86. [Speaking at Stationers Board of Trade dinner, New York, 10 Feb. 1887:] In my capacity of publisher I recently received a manuscript from a teacher which embodied a number of answers given by her pupils to questions propounded. These answers show that the children had nothing but the sound to go by; the sense was perfectly empty. Here are some of their answers to words they were asked to define: auriferous—pertaining to an orifice; ammonia—the food of the gods; equestrian—one who asks questions; parasite—a kind of umbrella; ipecac—a man who likes a good dinner. And here is the definition of an ancient word honored by a great party: Republican—a sinner mentioned in the Bible. And here is an innocent deliverance of a zoological kind: "There are a good many donkeys in the theological gardens." Here also is a definition which really isn't very bad in its way: demagogue—a vessel containing beer and other liquids.

Fatout, 217. MT published these with many more examples of boners from Caroline LeRow's *English as She Is Taught* (1887) in an anticipatory review, *Century* 33 (Apr. 1887): 932–36. His review formed the preface for the English edition of the book later that year.

87. [Retelling a story told by Chauncey Depew, 16 May 1887:] Greeley turned on the man who was collecting money to "save millions of your fellow creatures from going to hell": "I won't give you a d——d cent; there don't half enough of them go there *now*."

Notebook for Mar. 1886–June 1887; *N&J* 3: 290. Marshall Wilder, *Sunny Side of the Street* (1905), 137–38, also gives it as a favorite Depew story.

1887–1888

88. Fireman wants the widow to put off her son's funeral a day because the boys want to turn out on that day, & must lose the chance to turn out for *him* (a member) otherwise. The widow explains that the weather being warm, is afraid Jimmy won't keep.

The fire-laddie asks to examine the body—the weeping widow stands by: (Bends over body & snuffs.) Smf! smf! Sweet as a nut! —keep a week!

Notebook for Aug. 1887–July 1888; *N&J* 3: 302.

89. Rev. Alex Campbell, founder of the Campbellites, gently reproved our apprentice, Wales McCormick, on separate occasions, for saying Great God! when Great Scott would have done as well, & for committing the Unforgiven Sin when *any* other form of expression would have been a million times better. Weeks afterward, that inveterate light-head had his turn, & corrected the Reverend. In correcting the pamphlet-proof of one of Campbell's great sermons, Wales changed "Great God!" to "Great Scott," and changed Father, Son & Holy Ghost to Father, Son, & Caesar's Ghost. In overrunning, he reduced it to Father, Son & Co., to keep *from* overrunning. And Jesus *H.* Christ.

Notebook for Aug. 1887–July 1888; *N&J* 3: 305. MT and McCormick had been fellow apprentices on the *Missouri Courier,* Hannibal, where Campbell preached in Nov. 1852; Dixon Wecter, *SC of Hannibal* (1952), 308.

90. Father Adam & the apple—he didn't know it was loaded.

N&J 3: 306.

91. My abuse of somebody for telling me the most ancient of all humorous stories—then Tom Nast telling it that night at dinner—then Cable's hearing it at the reception in Buffalo— then next March when the President [Cleveland] was to arrive, I said something chaffingly about a "stranger always tells me that old tale if he is with me 15 minutes—don't be gone long." The President entered the one door as Cable stepped onto the stage from the other. Twenty minutes later, as I stepped onto the stage as Cable stepped off it, I was able to remark in his ear, "He told it to me."

Ibid., 308–309. Bernard L. Stein proposes that the old story was about "a humorous lecturer who flooded an ignorant audience with the killingest jokes for an hour and never got a laugh; and then when he was leaving, some gray simpletons wrung him gratefully by the hand and said it had been the funniest thing they had ever heard, and 'it was all they could do to keep from laughin' right aout in meetin!'" (*Connecticut Yankee* [1979], 123, 555). My own candidate would be the joke about Niagara Falls below, **117.**

1888

92. [A Finnish visitor records a MT anecdote:] A colored cook was just about to send the roast into the dining room when his sweetheart came to see him. The roast was a rare, juicy goose, and the girl cast longing glances at it. Temptation overcame the poor cook. He cut off one of the legs and gave it to his lady-love.

When the master began to carve the roast at the table, he immediately discovered the fraud. His brow clouded over, but he did not say anything. After dinner he went out into the kitchen and inquired for the chef. The cook approached, shivering with fear.

"Sam, how dare you pilfer the legs from my geese before you send them to the table?"

"I don't understand what you mean, massa."

"I'll teach you to understand. How did you dare cut off the leg of the goose which we had for dinner today?"

"I didn't cut it off, massa."

"Is that so? So you didn't cut it off? How come the goose had only one leg?"

"How—well—presumably it was created that way."

"Like that? You believe, then, that there are one-legged geese?"

"I believe so, massa."

"Well, good. Come with me."

The master and the cook stepped into the poultry yard, where the geese, turkeys, and hens vied with each other in gabbling. In a sunny corner several dozing geese stood on one leg and the cook immediately hastened to point them out to his master.

"So," said the master, "you think that they are created with only one leg. Well, we'll see."

He clapped his hands together and shouted, "Shoo!"
Immediately the legs came down and the geese waddled off,
cackling, on their two feet.
"Well?" said the master triumphantly.
"Well, but—I guess massa didn't shout 'shoo' to the roast."

Alexandra Gripenberg, *A Half Year in the New World* (1888), trans.
& ed. Ernest J. Moyne (1954), 70–71. In *AL* 45 (1973): 370–78, Moyne
shows how, when the baroness printed this story in Scandinavian newspapers, MT was accused of plagiarizing from Boccacio, he sent a rejoin-
der pointing out that the story came to him from F. Hopkinson Smith
and that it was fatuous to seek origins for such tales.

1888–1889

93. "And such a sight as he was,—" said she; "there he sat, almost stark naked—not a thing on but a pair of spectacles." Paused,
& added, musingly, "and one of *them* was broke, & you could
see him right through it."

Notebook for July 1888–May 1889; *N&J* 3: 410.

94. [Reporting his advice to Johns Hopkins University:] I told
them I believed they were perfectly competent to run a college,
as far as the higher branches of education are concerned, but what
they needed was a little help here & there from a practical commercial mind. I said the public are sensitive to little things, &
they wouldn't ever have full/solid confidence in a college that didn't
know how to spell John.

N&J 3: 456.

1889–1890

95. "He said he would rather sleep with Adelina Patti without
a stitch of clothes on than with General Grant in full uniform."

Notebook for May 1889–Aug. 1890; *N&J* 3: 537. James Montgomery
Flagg uses this in his autobiography as part of a dialogue between MT
and Howells; *Roses and Buckshot* (1946), 169.

96.   Dying man couldn't make up his mind which place to go to—both have their advantages, "heaven for climate, hell for company!"

Notebook for May 1889–Aug. 1890; *N&J* 3: 538. MT used this in a speech of 1901; *Speeches* (1910), 117. His physician, Dr. C.C. Rice, also recalled it as part of an anecdote about a favorite cigar maker: "He is dead, but I don't know which place he selected. Both places have their attractions—Heaven for Climate, and Hell for Society—but I think his punishment for making these cigars must be a sentence to the latter place"; *Mentor* 12 (1924): 48.

1890

97.   [Describing Christopher Columbus's return to Spain:] When he returned, the King of Spain, marveling, said—as history records:

"This ship seem to be leaky. Did she leak badly?"

"You shall judge for yourself, sire. I pumped the Atlantic ocean through her sixteen times on the passage."

This is General Horace Porter's account. Other authorities say fifteen.

"About All Kinds of Ships" [1890], *£1,000,000 Bank-note and Other New Stories* (1893), 175–76.

98.   [Recalling how, on the voyage from San Francisco to the Sandwich Islands, his ship was becalmed a fortnight in one spot:] Then a handsome breeze came fanning over the sea, and we spread our white wings for flight. But the vessel did not budge. The sails bellied out, the gale strained at the ropes, but the vessel moved not a hair's breadth from her place. The captain was surprised. It was some hours before we found out what the cause of the detention was. It was barnacles. They collect very fast in that part of the Pacific. They had fastened themselves to the ship's bottom; then others had fastened themselves to the first bunch, others to these, and so on, down and down and down, and the last bunch had glued the column hard and fast to the bottom of the sea, which is five miles deep at that point.

So the ship was simply become the handle of a walking cane five miles long—yes, and no more movable by wind and sail than a continent is. It was regarded by every one as remarkable.

Ibid., 182–83.

99. [Responding to an appeal for advice to young writers and explaining how reading develops a writer's clarity:] Well, also he will notice in the course of time, as his reading goes on, that the difference between the *almost right* word and the *right* word is really a large matter—'tis the difference between the lightning-bug and the lightning.

In George Bainton, *The Art of Authorship* (1890), 87–88. The *MTJ* reproduces a typescript captioned "To an unknown clergyman," dated 15 Oct. 1888; 18 (1977), outside back cover. MT used the figure again in a speech of 30 Nov. 1901: "Josh Billings defined the difference between humor and wit as that between the lightning bug and the lightning"; Fatout, 424. He also used it in the mock warning against onanism, **68** above.

1890–1891

100. Wm Penn achieved the deathless gratitude of the savages by merely dealing in a square way with them—well, kind of a square way, anyhow—more rectangular than the *savage* was used to, at any rate. He bought the whole State of Pa from them & paid for it like a man. Paid $40 worth of glass beads & a couple of second-hand blankets. Bought the whole State for that. Why you can't buy its *legislature* for twice the money now.

Notebook for Aug. 1890–June 1891: *N&J* 3: 589.

101. [Robert G.] Ingersoll's story of the man that went down from heaven on a reduced-rate excursion ticket good for 30 days —& tried to sell his return ticket.

N&J 3: 633. In the notebook for Mar.–Dec. 1895 the man is "a Presbyterian saint"; *MT's Notebook,* ed. Paine, 241.

102.   Bill Styles, lobbying in behalf of a candidate for U.S. Senator,— in the legislature. Spoke of the low grade of legislative morals.

"Kind of discouraging. You see, it's so hard to find men of a so high type of morals that they'll *stay bought.*"

N&J 3: 636.

103.   chastity-Harte

Ibid., 645. A memo for the story in manuscript (*MTE,* 269) expands the note to tell how Bret Harte as a young editor proofreading a newspaper corrected the word "chastity" by querying and underlining it for the printer's attention. The next morning's paper read: "Even in Yreka her *chastity* was conspicuous(?)" Harte's own version appeared in *Harper's Monthly* for May 1866 (32: 814), where the heroine was said to have been "'remarkable for her *chastity.*(?)'"

104.   A few days ago I called at the office of George Putnam, the publisher. I was met by a very severe-looking clerk, who told me that Mr. Putnam wasn't in. I knew that wasn't true, but I didn't blame the young man, for I don't think he liked the look of my clothes, but I thought as long as I had paid him a visit I would do some business with him, and I said I wanted to buy a book — a book of travel or something of that kind — and he handed me a volume which he said would cost three dollars. I said to him: "I am a publisher myself, and I suppose you allow the usual publisher's discount of 60 percent." The young man looked absent-minded, but said nothing. Then I remarked: "I am also an author, and I suppose you allow the usual author's discount of 30 percent." The young man looked pale. I addressed him further: "I also belong to the human race, and I suppose you allow the usual discount to the human race of 10 percent." The young man said nothing, but he took a pencil from behind his ear and made an arithmetical calculation and remarked: "After adding to that 5 percent discount for natural shyness, I find that the firm owes you fifteen cents."

Speech, Astor House, New York, 9 Oct. 1890; Fatout, 263–64.

1892

The next eight entries are from the first biography, *Mark Twain His Life and Work* (1892) by Will M. Clemens, no kin.

105. On one occasion Clemens was standing at the corner of Clay and Montgomery Streets, leaning against a lamp post and holding a cigar box under his arm. Mrs. Captain Edward Poole, a very beautiful woman, and as bright and witty as beautiful, came along and stopped and held out her hand, saying: "Why, Mark, where are you going in such a hurry?"

"I'm m-o-o-v-ing," drawled Mark, at the same time opening the cigar box disclosing a pair of blue socks, a pipe and two paper collars.

Pp. 59–60.

106. One day a comedian from a local theatre approached Mark on the street:

"See here, Clemens," said he, "I need a half-dozen good jokes. Get 'em up and I'll give you five dollars."

"Sorry, old man," answered Mark, thoughtfully, "but I'm afraid the scheme won't work."

"Why not?"

"Well, the fact is, I'm so d——d poor, if I was found with $5 on my person people would say I stole them; on the other hand, if you got off any decent jokes people would say you stole them, too."

Pp. 67–68.

107. [Desiring to know if MT's intentions toward his daughter are honorable, his prospective father-in-law asks him for references, and Mark puts on "a bold front:"]

"Sir," said he, bowing profoundly, as became a young man who respects his hoped-for father-in-law, "your sentiments are in every way correct. I approve of them myself, and hasten to add that you have not been mistaken in my sentiments towards your daughter, whom I may tell you candidly seems to me to be the most

perfect of her sex, and I honor your solicitation for her welfare.
I am not only perfectly willing to give you reference, but am only
too glad to have an opportunity to do so, which my natural modesty would have prevented me from offering. Therefore, permit
me to give you the names of a few of my friends. I will write them
down. First is Lieutenant General John McComb, Alexander Bad-
lam, General Lander and Col. W.H.L. Barnes. They will all lie
for me just as I would for them under like circumstances."

Pp. 104–105.

108.   The Reverend J. Hyatt Smith relates an amusing anecdote of Mark's life in Buffalo: "When I was living in Buffalo,"
says Mr. Smith, "Mark Twain occupied a cottage across the street.
We did not see very much of him, but one morning as we were
enjoying our cigars on the veranda after breakfast, we saw Mark
come to his door in his dressing-gown and slippers, and look over
at us. He stood at his own door and smoked for a minute, as if
making up his mind about something, and, at last, opened his
gate and came lounging across the street. There was an unoccu-
pied rocking-chair on the veranda, and when my brother offered
it to him he dropped into it with a sigh of relief. He smoked
for a few moments and said:
"Nice morning."
"Yes, very pleasant."
"Shouldn't wonder if we had rain by and by."
"Well, we could stand a little."
"This is a nice house you have here?"
"Yes, we rather like it."
"How's your family?"
"Quite well — and yours?"
"Oh, we're comfortable."
There was another impressive silence, and finally Mark crossed
his legs, blew a puff of smoke in the air, and in his lazy drawl,
remarked:
"'I suppose you're a little surprised to see me over here so early.
Fact is, I haven't been so neighborly, perhaps, as I ought to be.
We must mend that state of things. But this morning I came over

because I thought you might be interested in knowing that your roof is on fire. . . .'"

Pp. 107–109. There must be something to this story since it is repeated by both MT's minister and doctor; Rev. J.H. Twichell, *Harper's Monthly* 92 (May 1896): 821; Dr. C.C. Rice, *Mentor* 12 (May 1924): 56.

109. Mr. Clemens met with an amusing adventure when he and Mr. Cable were making their tour in the South. A misguided but enthusiastic young man managed, after some difficulty, to secure an introduction to the humorist on a river steamer, just before the latter's departure from New Orleans for St. Louis. The young man said: "I've read all of your writings, Mr. Twain, but I think I like 'The Heathen Chinee' the best of them all." Mr. Clemens shook the young man's hand with tremendous enthusiasm. "My dear sir," he remarked, "I am pretty well used to compliments, but I must say I never received one which gave me equal satisfaction, and showed so kindly an appreciation of efforts to please the public. A thousand thanks." And the young man replied, "You are perfectly welcome, Mr. Twain. I am sure you deserve it."

Pp. 155–56. This scene from another view appeared in *Harper's Weekly*, 23 Dec. 1905. George W. Cable reminded MT that the young man later confessed to a friend: "I, I was so embarrassed—I—I've read everything he ever wrote and I would thank him for every one of them, and when I got hold of his hand my heart was so big that the only thing I could think of his to thank him for was the 'Heathen Chinee,'" which of course was Bret Harte's classic (49:1888).

110. [Welcoming a military regiment from Worcester, Massachusetts to Hartford:] One reason I didn't like to come here to make a prepared speech was because I have sworn off. I have reformed. I would not make a prepared speech without statistics and philosophy. The advantage of a prepared speech is that you start when you are ready and stop when you get through. If unprepared, you are all at sea, you don't know where you are. I thought to achieve brevity, but I was mistaken. A man never hangs on so long on his hind legs as when he don't know when to stop. I once heard a man who tried to be reformed. He tried to be brief.

A number of strangers sat in a hotel parlor. One sat off to one side and said nothing. Finally all went out except one man and this dummy. The dummy touched this man on the shoulder and said: "I think I have s-s-s-e (whistles) een you before." "What makes you whistle?" asked the other man. "I used to stammer, and the d-d-d-d- (whistles) octor told me when I w-w-w-w-w- (whistles) anted to speak and s-s-s-s-tammered to whistle. I d-d-d- (whistle) id whistle and it c-c-c-c-ured me."

Pp. 158–59.

111. It is said that once when Mr. Clemens, at the solicitation of his wife, called on Mrs. [Harriet Beecher] Stowe, he was so absent-minded as to put on neither collar nor necktie. On Mrs. Clemens remonstrating on his return, he said he would make it all right, and accordingly sent a collar and tie of his over to Mrs. Stowe in a box.

P. 181.

112. At a Hartford dinner party one day, the subject of eternal life and future punishment came up for a lengthy discussion, in which Mark Twain, who was present took no part. A lady near him turned suddenly toward him and exclaimed:

"Why do you not say anything? I want your opinion."

Mr. Clemens replied gravely: "Madam, you must excuse me. I am silent of necessity. I have friends in both places."

Pp. 187–88.

113. A use has been found for everything but snoring.

Notebook for May 1892–Jan. 1893, MTP, 46.

1893

114. [A fellow newspaper man reminisces about MT's career in Virginia City:] He and the Episcopal clergyman became friends, and while the clergyman probably did not consider Sam a devout Christian, at least he regarded him as a promising young

man whose leanings were in the right direction. Now, the printers knew that to steal the shade of Mr. Clemens' lamp caused
him to burn with a slow fury. So they stole it as often as they
could for the pleasure of hearing him swear—an art in which he
excelled. One evening at dusk he climbed to the deserted local
room and found the shade gone. Thereupon he began to drag
himself around in a leisurely but intense circle, as was his wont
on such occasions, uttering oaths and calling down heaven's vengeance on the purloiners. While thus breathing maledictions he
passed the door and beheld the Episcopal minister standing therein
transfixed with horror.

Mark paused not in his slow walk, but had the grace to drawl
out in low ferocity this (expurgated) excuse:

"I know you're shocked to hear me, Mr. Brown. It stands to
reason you are. I know this ain't language fit for a Christian man
to utter nor for a Christian man to hear, but if I could only lay
my hands on the ——— — ——— — — ——— ——— who stole
my shade, I'd show you what I'd do to him, for the benefit of
printers to all time. You don't know printers, Mr. Brown; you
don't know them. A Christian man like you naturally can't come
in contact with them, but I give you my word they're the ———
——— ——— ——— that a body ever had anything
to do with."

Arthur McEwen, "Heroic Days on the Comstock," San Francisco *Examiner*, 22 Jan. 1893; O. Lewis, ed., *Territorial Enterprise* (1971), 34–35.

115.   [Another colleague and former roommate reminisces about
those days:] A good deal has been said first and last of the steal-
ing of Tom Fitch's firewood while Mark and I were rooming at the
Daggett & Meyers building. Tom never lost much wood through
us, but the boys would always have it otherwise. Wood was something of an object in those days, as in winter it sometimes boomed
up to $40 a cord. We were in the habit of buying of the Chinese
wood-peddlers by the donkey load. One bitterly cold night we
found ouselves without wood. In the hall on the same floor stood
Tom's well filled wood box. Said Mark: "We are not going to freeze
in here with plenty of wood just outside our door," and out he

went and gathered up an armful of Tom's wood. Coming back
to our door he threw a stick of wood upon the floor and made
a great racket. This was to arouse Tom. Then, opening the door
with a bang, he faced about in it as if he had just come from
the inside and sang out in an angry tone, as though to me in
the hall: "Dan, d——n it all, don't be taking Tom's wood! It ain't
right, and wood so confounded high! It ain't a nice thing to do.
Now take that wood right back or there'll be trouble!"

He then went back to the wood box and made a big racket,
but when he threw down one stick he picked up two, and presently he came into the room with wood piled up to his chin.
This he put down so carefully that the sticks wouldn't have broken
an egg. We soon had a rousing fire and wood to spare for the
morning.

William Wright (Dan de Quille), "Salad Days of MT," San Francisco
Examiner, 19 Mar. 1893; O. Lewis, ed., *Territorial Enterprise*, 39–40.

116.   Virginia City was booming when Artemus Ward arrived
to deliver his lecture. Comstockers received Artemus as a brother,
and he seemed as much at home as if he had all his life been
a resident of Virginia City. He remained on the Comstock several
days, making the *Enterprise* his headquarters. Mark Twain and
I had the pleasure of showing him the town, and a real pleasure
it was—a sort of circus, in fact,—as he constantly overflowed with
fun. He was anxious to get hold of the lingo and style of the miners, and we made him acquainted with several old forty-niners.
The greetings among these men struck him as something new,
and he began practicing, playing himself off as an old-timer. The
looks of astonishment which his efforts in this line called up in
some quarters soon showed him that the half-horse half-alligator
style of greeting was only good with a certain class. Mark Twain
had a weakness for the clergy, and meeting one of his preacher
friends on the street one day he introduced him to Ward without
adding to the name the handle of "Reverend." Some twinkle in
the eye of the reverend gentleman caused Artemus to think him
one of the "old boys," so he greeted him with: "Well, old Two-
Pan-One-Color, is the devil still in your dough-dish?"

Mark hastened to explain, and it all ended in a laugh, in which Ward joined very faintly.

William Wright; O. Lewis, ed., *Territorial Enterprise*, 46–47.

117. [From Adam's diary:] TEN DAYS LATER. — She accuses *me* of being the cause of our disaster! She says, with apparent sincerity and truth, that the Serpent assured her that the forbidden fruit was not apples, it was chestnuts. I said I was innocent, then, for I had not eaten any chestnuts. She said the Serpent informed her that "chestnut" was a figurative term meaning an aged and mouldy joke. I turned pale at that, for I have made many jokes to pass the weary time, and some of them could have been of that sort, though I had honestly supposed they were new when I made them. She asked me if I had made one just at the time of the catastrophe. I was obliged to admit that I had made one to myself, though not aloud. It was this. I was thinking about the Falls, and I said to myself, "How wonderful it is to see that vast body of water tumble down there!" Then in an instant a bright thought flashed into my head, and I let it fly, saying, "It would be a deal more wonderful to see it tumble *up* there!" — and I was about to kill myself with laughing at it when all nature broke loose in war and death and I had to flee for my life. "There," she said, with triumph, "that is just it; the Serpent mentioned that very jest, and called it the First Chestnut, and said it was coeval with the creation."

"Extracts from Adam's Diary," *The Niagara Book* (1893), 101–102. This was "a complete souvenir of Niagara Falls containing sketches, stories. . . . written exclusively for this book by W.D. Howells, Mark Twain, Prof. Nathaniel S. Shaler, and Others" and published at Buffalo.

118. [From a letter to H.H. Rogers, complaining about the "hotel d'Angleterre":] We are on the second floor from the ground. There's a W.C. on the floor *above* us and one on the floor *below* us. Halls pitch dark. I groped my way and found the upper W.C. Starting to return, I went up stairs instead of down, and went to what I supposed was my room, but I could not make out the number in the dark and was afraid to enter it. Then I remembered that I — no, my mind lost confidence and began to wander. I was no longer sure as to what floor I was on, and the minute I realized that, the rest of my mind went. One cannot stand still in a dark hall at two in the morning, lost, and be content. One must move and go on moving, even at the risk of getting worse lost. I groped up and down a couple of those flights, over and over again, cursing to myself. And every time I thought I heard somebody coming, I shrank together like one of those toy balloons when it collapses. You see, I was between two fires; I could not grope to the top floor and start fresh and count down to my own, for it was all occupied by young ladies and a dangerous place to get caught in, clothed as I was clothed, and not in my right mind. I could not grope down to the ground floor and count *up,* for there was a ball down there. A ball, and young ladies likely to be starting up to bed about this time. And so they were. I saw the glow of their distant candle, I felt the chill of their distant cackle. I did not know whether I was on a W.C. floor or not, but I had to take a risk. I groped to the door that ought to be it — right where you turn down the stairs; and it was it. I entered it grateful, and stood in its dark shelter with a beating heart and thought how happy I should be to live there always; in that humble cot, and go out no more among life's troubles and dangers. Several of the young ladies applied for admission, but I was not receiving. Thursdays being my day. I meant to freeze out the ball if it took a week. And I did. When the drone and burr of its music had ceased for twenty mintues and the house was solidly dead and dark, I groped down the ground floor, then turned and counted my way up home, all right.

Then straightway my temper went up to 180 in the shade and I began to put it into form. Presently an admiring voice said — "When you are through with your prayers, I would like to ask where you have been, all night."

MT's Notebook, ed. Paine, 239–40.

119.   He was perfectly frank about it and said he wanted to go to hell: said he had got used to reading the (Paris [edition of the]) N.Y. Herald and couldn't do without it.

Ibid.

The next twelve entries are from the advertising pamphlet *Pudd'n-head Wilson's Calendar for 1894,* issued in 1893 to herald the serial appearance of the novel in the *Century Magazine.* The maxims prefacing the individual chapters in the *Century* appear in a second group of entries, and a third consists of maxims that were added to the novel and that were not in the *Century.*

120. January—Nothing so needs reforming as other people's habits.

121. February—Behold the fool saith, "Put not all thine eggs in the one basket," which is but a manner of saying, "Scatter your money and your attention," but the wise man saith, put all thine eggs in the one basket and—*watch that basket.*

A notebook entry, Apr. 1893, attributed the saying to Andrew Carnegie, perhaps in jest. *MT's Notebook,* ed. Paine, 231.

122. March—When angry, count a hundred; when very angry, swear.

The printer had unfortunately changed MT's "four" to "a hundred," defeating the burlesque; MT demanded a second printing to correct the error. It read "four" in the *Century* for February (47: 551).

123. April—April 1st: This is the day upon which we are reminded of what we are on the other three hundred and sixty-four.

124. May—It were not best that we should all think alike; it is difference of opinion that makes horse-races.

125. June—When I reflect upon the number of disagreeable people who I know have gone to a better world, I am moved to lead a different life.

126. July—July 4th: Statistics show that we lose more fools on this day than in all the other days of the year put together. This proves, by the number left in stock, that one Fourth of July per year is now inadequate, the country has grown so.

Cartoon courtesy of Watterson, copyright © 1983 by the *Mark Twain Journal*.

127. August—Why is it that we rejoice at a birth and grieve at a funeral? Is it because we are not the person involved?

In *The Tragedy of Pudd'nhead Wilson* (1894) the second question appears as a declaration.

128. September—If you pick up a starving dog and make him prosperous, he will not bite you. This is the principal difference between a dog and a man.

In a draft, notebook 32, p. 46, the first sentence continues, "but stop with the dog; don't try it with a man," which was crossed out.

129. October—This is one of the peculiarly dangerous months to speculate in stocks in. The others are July, January, September, April, November, May, March, June, December, August and February.

130. November—Few things are harder to put up with than the annoyance of a good example.

131. December—Even the clearest and most perfect circumstantial evidence is likely to be at fault, after all, and therefore ought to be received with great caution.—Take the case of any pencil sharpened by any woman: if you have witnesses, you will find she did it with a knife; but if you take simply the aspect of the pencil, you will say she did it with her teeth.

The next fifteen entries are from the serial "Pudd'nhead Wilson," *Century Magazine,* Dec. 1893–June 1894, which also included the maxims appearing in the *Calendar* given above but not reprinted here.

132. There is no character, howsoever good and fine, but it can be destroyed by ridicule, howsoever poor and witless. Observe the ass, for instance: his character is about perfect, he is the choicest spirit among all the humbler animals, yet see what ridicule has brought him to. Instead of feeling complimented when we are called an ass, we are left in doubt.

47 (Dec. 1893): 233.

133. Tell the truth or trump—but get the trick.

Ibid.

134. Adam was but human—this explains it all. He did not want the apple for the apple's sake, he wanted it only because it was forbidden. The mistake was in not forbidding the serpent; then he would have eaten the serpent.

Ibid., 235. Notebook 35, p. 45, has a draft of this maxim concluding: "If he had really cared for us he would have thought of this himself," which was deleted.

1894

135. Adam and Eve had many advantages, but the principal one was, that they escaped teething.

47 (Jan. 1894): 329.

136.   There is this trouble about special providences—namely, there is so often a doubt as to which party was intended to be the benficiary. In the case of the children, the bears and the prophet, the bears got more real satisfaction out of the episode than the prophet did, because they got the children.

Ibid. In 2 Kings 2:24 the bears eat forty-two of the children who had been teasing prophet Elisha.

137.   It is easy to find fault, if one has that disposition. There was once a man who, not being able to find any other fault with his coal, complained that there were too many prehistoric toads in it.

47 (Feb. 1894): 549

138.   There are three infallible ways of pleasing an author, and the three form a rising scale of compliment: 1, to tell him you have read one of his books; 2, to tell him you have read all of his books; 3, to ask him to let you read the manuscript of his forthcoming book. No. 1 admits you to his respect; No. 2 admits you to his admiration; No. 3 carries you clear into his heart.

Ibid., 552.

139.   As to the Adjective: when in doubt, strike it out.

Ibid.

140.   The true Southern watermelon is a boon apart, and not to be mentioned with commoner things. It is chief of this world's luxuries, king by the grace of God over all the fruits of the earth. When one has tasted it, he knows what the angels eat. It was not a Southern watermelon that Eve took: we know it because she repented.

47 (Mar. 1894): 777.

141.   Even popularity can be overdone. In Rome, along at first, you are full of regrets that Michelangelo died; but by and by you only regret that you didn't see him do it.

47 (Apr. 1894): 821.

142. Gratitude and treachery are merely the two extremities of the same procession. You have seen all of it that is worth staying for when the band and the gaudy officials have gone by.

48 (May 1894): 17.

143. Thanksgiving Day. Let all give humble, hearty, and sincere thanks, now, but the turkeys. In the island of Fiji they do not use turkeys; they use plumbers. It does not become you and me to sneer at Fiji.

Ibid.

144. He is useless on top of the ground; he ought to be under it, inspiring the cabbages.

48 (June 1894): 235.

145. It is often the case that the man who can't tell a lie thinks he is the best judge of one.

Ibid. 240.

146. It was wonderful to find America, but it would have been more wonderful to miss it.

Ibid.

147. In the first place God made idiots. This was for practice. Then he made proofreaders.

Notebook, May 1892–Jan. 1893, MTP, 43. For variants, see **230** and **497**. These are discussed in William Gibson, *The Art of MT* (1976), 169.

The next eleven entries are from the book *The Tragedy of Pudd'nhead Wilson and the Comedy of the Extraordinary Twins,* published 28 Nov. 1894. Previously published maxims are not repeated below.

148. Whoever has lived long enough to find out what life is, knows how deep a debt of gratitude we owe to Adam, the first great benefactor of our race. He brought death into the world.

Ch. 3, p. 41. For variant, see **313.**

149. Training is everything. The peach was once a bitter almond; cauliflower is nothing but cabbage with a college education.

Ch. 5, p. 67.

150. Remark of Dr. [William] Baldwin's, concerning upstarts: We don't care to eat toadstools that think they are truffles.

Ibid. I assume the allusion is to Dr. William Baldwin (1779–1819), physician and botanist who died on the expedition exploring the Missouri River. His scientific letters were edited by William Darlington in 1843, *Reliquae Baldwinianae,* ed. Joseph Ewan (1969).

151. Let us endeavor so to live that when we come to die even the undertaker will be sorry.

Ch. 6, p. 77.

152. Habit is habit, and not to be flung out of the window by any man, but coaxed down-stairs a step at a time.

Ibid.

153. One of the most striking differences between a cat and a lie is that a cat has only nine lives.

Ch. 9, p. 86.

154. The holy passion of Friendship is of so sweet and steady and loyal and enduring a nature that it will last through a whole lifetime, if not asked to lend money.

Ch. 8, p. 93.

155. Consider well the proportion of things. It is better to be a young June-bug than an old bird of paradise.

Ch. 8, p. 93.

156.   All say, "How hard it is that we have to die"—a strange complaint to come from the mouths of people who have had to live.

Ch. 10, p. 121.

157.   Courage is resistance to fear, mastery of fear—not absence of fear. . . . When we speak of [Robert] Clive, [Horatio] Nelson, and [Israel] Putnam as men who "didn't know what fear was," we ought always to add the flea—and put him at the head of the procession.

Ch. 12, p. 155.

158.   We know all about the habits of the ant, we know all about the habits of the bee, but we know nothing at all about the habits of the oyster. It seems almost certain that we have been choosing the wrong time for studying the oyster.

Ch. 16, p. 214.

159.   [A French reporter in Paris records an impromptu performance:] To give us a glimpse into the American character, Mr. Twain invented offhand the following whimsical anecdote:

An American, crossing a bridge in Paris, the bridge of the Concorde, for example, stops and looks curiously at a fisherman with his line, seated placidly on the embankment and in the process of luring hypothetical fish. For a good quarter of an hour, the tourist observes the stratagems of the fisherman, and as they are always without result, the American decides to descend to the embankment. He inquires of the fisherman in bad French:

"Oho! my boy, what are you doing there?"

The fisherman turns without emotion: "Me? I am fishing," he replies.

The American retorts: "No, you are there in order to fish, and you aren't fishing up anything at all . . . *indeed.* If you don't catch anything in five minutes, I am going to throw you in the river."

The fisherman, thinking this is a joke, goes back to casting his line, still without success. The American, remaining behind him, pulls out his watch. The five minutes elapse. The fisherman has caught nothing. Then, without warning him a second time, the American gives him a push; the man disappears and the tourist goes off whistling, happy to have suppressed a useless individual.

Gabriel Randon, "MT," Paris *Figaro,* 5 Apr. 1894; rpt. L.J. Budd, "Interviews with MT," *ALR* 10 (1977): 50.

1895

160.   In our country several years ago there was a man came into a prohibition town . . . and they said to him, "You can't get a drink anywhere except at the apothecary's." So he went to the apothecary, who said, "You can't get a drink here without a prescription from a physician," but the man said, "I'm perishing. I haven't had time to get a prescription." The apothecary replied, "Well, I haven't power to give you a drink except for snake bite." The man said, "Where's the snake?" So the apothecary gave him the snake's address, and he went off. Soon after, however, he came back and said, "For goodness' sake, give me a drink. That snake is engaged for months ahead."

Speech at Christchurch, New Zealand, 15 Nov. 1895; Fatout, 303.

1896

161.   Swore off from profanity early this morning. I was on deck in the peaceful dawn, the calm and holy dawn. Went down dressed, bathed, put on white linen, shaved—a long, hot, troublesome job, and no profanity. Then started to breakfast. Remembered my tonic—first time in three months without being told—poured it in a measuring-glass, held bottle in one hand, it in the other, the cork in my teeth—reached up and got a tumbler—measuring-glass sprang out of my fingers—got it, poured out another dose, first setting the tumbler on washstand—just got it poured, ship lurched, heard a crash behind me—it was the tumbler, broken into millions of fragments, but the bottom hunk whole—picked it up to throw out of the open port, threw out the measuring-glass instead—then I released my voice. Mrs. C. behind me in the door: "Don't reform any more, it isn't any improvement."

MT's Notebook, ed. Paine, 268, dated Jan. 1896.

162. [An Australian claims that his train was so slow he advised the conductor to put the cowcatcher on the other end of the train—] "Because we are not going to overtake any cows but there's no protection against their climbing aboard at the other end & biting the passengers."

Ibid., 299.

1897

163. Came Mr. [Frank M.] White, representing N.Y. Journal with two cablegrams from his paper.

One (1) "If Mark Twain dying in poverty, in London, send 500 words."

(2) "Later. If Mark Twain has died in poverty send 1000 words."

I explained how the mistake occurred and gave him a cable in substance this:

"James Ross Clemens, a cousin, was seriously ill here two or three weeks ago, but is well now. The report of my illness grew out of his illness; the report of my death was an exaggeration. I have not been ill. Mark Twain."

Ibid., 327–28, dated "Jan. 2, '97." A facsimile of the "cable" in MT's hand is the frontispiece of Cyril Clemens, MT's Jest Book (1963).

164. [When his wife hesitates to admit an interviewer because MT is abed:] "I said to her, 'Show him up, send some cigars up. I am comfortable enough!'

"'Yes,' she said, 'But what about him?'

"'Oh,' I said, 'if you want him to be as comfortable as I am make him up a bed in the other corner of the room.'"

N.Y. Herald, 6 June 1897; Merle Johnson, Bibliography, 147. In Vancouver, 17 Aug. 1895, he invited reporters to interview him while he was abed; James B. Pond, Eccentricities of Genius (1900), 221–22.

The next seventy-one entries are the maxims serving as headnotes for chapters of *Following the Equator* (1897), as from "Pudd'nhead Wilson's New Calendar."

165.   Be good and you will be lonesome.

Frontispiece.

166.   These wisdoms are for the luring of youth toward high moral altitudes. The author did not gather them from practice, but from observations. To be good is noble; but to show others how to be good is nobler and no trouble.

Preface.

167.   A man may have no bad habits and have worse.

Ch. 1, p. 25.

168.   When in doubt, tell the truth.

Ch. 2, p. 35.

169.   It is more trouble to make a maxim than it is to do right.

Ch. 3, p. 48. P. 49 reproduces the manscript of this maxim, showing that the word "trouble" began as "diffi" and the word "make" as "construct."

170.   A dozen direct censures are easier to bear than one morganatic compliment.

Ch. 4, p. 65.

171.   Noise proves nothing. Often a hen who has merely laid an egg cackles as if she had laid an asteroid.

Ch. 5, p. 77.

172.   He was as shy as a newspaper is when referring to its own merits.

Ch. 6, p. 83.

" IT COULD PROBABLY BE
SHOWN BY FACTS AND
FIGURES THAT THERE IS
NO DISTINCTLY NATIVE
AMERICAN CRIMINAL
CLASS EXCEPT CONGRESS."

— Pudd'nhead Wilson's
New Calendar

Cartoon courtesy of Watterson, copyright © 1983 by the *Mark Twain Journal*.

173. Truth is the most valuable thing we have. Let us economize it.

Ch. 7, p. 91.

174. It could probably be shown by facts and figures that there is no distinctly native American criminal class except Congress.

Ch. 8, p. 99.

175. It is your human environment that makes climate.

Ch. 9, p. 109.

176. Everything human is pathetic. The secret source of Humor itself is not joy but sorrow. There is no humor in heaven.

Ch. 10, p. 119.

177. We should be careful to get out of an experience only the wisdom that is in it — and stop there; lest we be like the cat that sits down on a hot stove-lid. She will never sit down on a hot stove-lid again — and that is well; but also she will never sit down on a cold one any more.

Ch. 11, p. 124.

178. There are those who scoff at the schoolboy, calling him frivolous and shallow. Yet it was the schoolboy who said "Faith is believing what you know ain't so."

Ch. 12, p. 132.

179. The timid man yearns for full value and asks a tenth. The bold man strikes for double value and compromises on par.

Ch. 13, p. 136.

180. We can secure other people's approval, if we do right and try hard; but our own is worth a hundred of it, and no way has been found out of securing that.

Ch. 14, p. 151.

181. Truth is stranger than fiction — to some people, but I am measurably familiar with it. Truth is stranger than fiction, but it is because Fiction is obliged to stick to possibilities; Truth isn't.

Ch. 15, p. 156.

182. There is a Moral Sense, and there is an Immoral Sense. History shows us that the Moral Sense enables us to perceive morality and how to avoid it, and that the Immoral Sense enables us to perceive immorality and how to enjoy it.

Ch. 16, p. 161.

183. The English are mentioned in the Bible: Blessed are the meek, for they shall inherit the earth.

Ch. 17, p. 170.

184. It is easier to stay out than get out.

Ch. 18, p. 176.

185.   Pity is for the living, envy is for the dead.

Ch. 19, p. 184.

186.   It is by the goodness of God that in our country we have those three unspeakably precious things: freedom of speech, freedom of conscience, and the prudence never to practice either of them.

Ch. 20, p. 195.

187.   Man will do many things to get himself loved, he will do all things to get himself envied.

Ch. 21, p. 206.

188.   Nothing is so ignorant as a man's left hand, except a lady's watch.

Ch. 22, p. 214.

189.   Be careless in your dress if you must, but keep a tidy soul.

Ch. 23, p. 223.

190.   There is no such thing as "the Queen's English." The property has gone into the hands of a joint stock company and we own the bulk of the shares!

Ch. 24, p. 230.

191.   "Classic." A book which people praise and don't read.

Ch. 25, p. 241.

192.   There are people who can do all fine and heroic things but one! keep from telling their happinesses to the unhappy.

Ch. 26, p. 251.

193.   Man is the Only Animal that Blushes. Or needs to.

Ch. 27, p. 256.

194. The universal brotherhood of man is our most precious possession, what there is of it.

Ibid.

195. Let us be thankful for the fools. But for them the rest of us could not succeed.

Ch. 28, p. 268.

196. When people do not respect us we are sharply offended; yet deep down in his private heart no man much respects himself.

Ch. 29, p. 279.

197. Nature makes the locust with an appetite for crops; man would have made him with an appetite for sand.

Ch. 30, p. 285.

198. The spirit of wrath — not the words — is the sin; and the spirit of wrath is cursing. We begin to swear before we can talk.

Ch. 31, p. 290.

199. The man with a new idea is a Crank until the idea succeeds.

Ch. 32, p. 297.

200. Let us be grateful to Adam our benefactor. He cut us out of the "blessing" of idleness and won for us the "curse" of labor.

Ch. 33, p. 305.

201. Let us not be too particular. It is better to have old second-hand diamonds than none at all.

Ch. 34, p. 312.

202. The Autocrat of Russia possesses more power than any other man in the earth; but he cannot stop a sneeze.

Ch. 35, p. 318.

203.   There are several good protections against temptations, but the surest is cowardice.

Ch. 36, p. 324.

204.   Names are not always what they seem. The common Welsh name Bzjxxllwcp is pronounced Jackson.

Ibid.

205.   To succeed in the other trades, capacity must be shown; in the law, concealment of it will do.

Ch. 37, p. 331.

206.   Prosperity is the best protector of principle.

Ch. 38, p. 345.

207.   By trying we can easily learn to endure adversity. Another man's, I mean.

Ch. 39, p. 357.

208.   Few of us can stand prosperity. Another man's I mean.

Ch. 40, p. 369.

209.   There is an old time toast which is golden for its beauty. "When you ascend the hill of prosperity may you not meet a friend."

Ch. 41, p. 379.

210.   Each person is born to one possession which outvalues all his others—his last breath.

Ch. 42, p. 386.

211.   Hunger is the handmaid of genius.

Ch. 43, p. 392.

212.   The old saw says, "Let a sleeping dog lie." Right. Still, when there is much at stake it is better to get a newspaper to do it.

Ch. 44, p. 400.

213.   It takes your enemy and your friend, working together, to hurt you to the heart; the one to slander you and the other to get the news to you.

Ch. 45, p. 410.

214.   If the desire to kill and the opportunity to kill came always together, who would escape hanging?

Ch. 46, p. 426. In an interview with the New York *Herald,* 6 June 1897, he applied this saying to charity: "If the impulse to kill and the opportunity to kill always came at the same instant, how many of us would escape hanging"; Merle Johnson, *Bibliography,* 149.

215.   Simple rules for saving money: To save half, when you are fired by an eager impulse to contribute to a charity, wait, and count forty. To save three-quarters, count sixty. To save it all, count sixty-five.

Ch. 47, p. 437.

216.   Grief can take care of itself; but to get the full value of a joy you must have somebody to divide it with.

Ch. 48, p. 447.

217.   He had had much experience of physicians, and said, "the only way to keep your health is to eat what you don't want, drink what you don't like, and do what you'd druther not."

Ch. 49, p. 459.

218.   The man who is ostentatious of his modesty is twin to the statue that wears a fig-leaf.

Ch. 50, p. 475.

219. Let me make the superstitions of a nation and I care not who makes its laws or its songs either.

Ch. 51, p. 484.

220. Wrinkles should merely indicate where smiles have been.

Ch. 52, p. 496.

221. True irreverence is disrespect for another man's god.

Ch. 53, p. 507.

222. Do not undervalue the headache. While it is at its sharpest it seems a bad investment; but when relief begins, the unexpired remainder is worth $4 a minute.

Ch. 54, p. 517.

223. There are 869 different forms of lying, but only one of them has been squarely forbidden. Thou shalt not bear false witness against thy neighbor.

Ch. 55, p. 524. In the notebook of May 1892–Jan. 1893 this is the conclusion of a long paragraph on the commandment to multiply and replenish the earth. Of the 417 commandments, MT says, "Only a single one of the 417 has found ministerial obedience; multiply &c. To it sinner & saint, scholar & ignoramus, Christian & savage are alike loyal"; MTP, 44.

224. There are two times in a man's life when he should not speculate: when he can't afford it, and when he can.

Ch. 56, p. 535.

225. She was not quite what you would call refined. She was not what you would call unrefined. She was the kind of person that keeps a parrot.

Ch. 57, p. 544.

226. Make it a point to do something every day that you don't want to do. This is the golden rule for acquiring the habit of doing your duty without pain.

Ch. 58, p. 549.

227.   Don't part with your illusions. When they are gone you may still exist but you have ceased to live.

Ch. 59, p. 567.

228.   Often, the surest way to convey misinformation is to tell the strict truth.

Ibid.

229.   *Satan* (impatiently) to *New-Comer.* The trouble with you Chicago people is, that you think you are the best people down here; whereas you are merely the most numerous.

Ch. 60, p. 582.

230.   In the first place God made idiots. This was for practice. Then He made School Boards.

Ch. 61, p. 597.

231.   There are no people who are quite so vulgar as the over-refined ones.

Ch. 62, p. 609.

232.   The principal difference between a cat and a lie is that the cat has only nine lives.

Ch. 63, p. 622. Variant of **153**, headnote to ch. 9 of *Pudd'nhead Wilson.*

233.   When your watch gets out of order you have choice of two things to do: throw it in the fire or take it to the watch-tinker. The former is the quickest.

Ch. 64, p. 630.

234. In statesmanship get the formalities right, never mind about the moralities.

Ch. 65, p. 644.

235. Every one is a moon, and has a dark side which he never shows to anybody.

Ch. 66, p. 654.

236. First catch your Boer, then kick him.

Ch. 67, p. 667. Opposed to the Boer War (1899–1902), MT joked about the "succession of brilliant British victories, which always leave the Boers on top"; *MT-Howells Letters*, 2: 714.

237. None of us can have as many virtues as the fountain-pen, or half its cussedness; but we can try.

Ch. 68, p. 686.

238. The very ink with which all history is written is merely fluid prejudice.

Ch. 69, p. 699.

239. There isn't a Parallel of Latitude but thinks it would have been the Equator if it had had its rights.

Ibid.

240. I have traveled more than any one else, and I have noticed that even the angels speak English with an accent.

Conclusion, p. 710.

1898

The next thirty-seven entries are from the notebook of 1898 in *MT's Notebook*, ed. Paine, 343–47.

241. Some men worship rank, some worship heroes, some wor-

ship power, some worship God, and over these ideals they dispute
—but they all worship money.

242. To ask a doctor's opinion of osteopathy is equivalent to
going to Satan for information about Christianity.

243. You can't depend on your judgment when your imagination is out of focus.

244. The proper office of a friend is to side with you when
you are in the wrong. Nearly anybody will side with you when
you are in the right.

245. God's inhumanity to man makes countless thousands
mourn.

The parody is of Robert Burns's "Man's inhumanity to Man / Makes
countless thousands mourn!"; "Man Was Made to Mourn," *Poems &
Songs,* ed. James Kinsley (1968), 1: 118.

246. Of the demonstrably wise there are but two; those who
commit suicide, and those who keep their reasoning faculties
atrophied with drink.

247. The radical of one century is the conservative of the next.
The radical invents the views. When he has worn them out the
conservative adopts them.

248. There has been only one Christian. They caught Him and
crucified Him early.

249. What God lacks is convictions—stability of character. He
ought to be a Presbyterian or a Catholic or *something*—not try
to be everything.

250. If all men were rich, all men would be poor.

251. Let us swear while we may, for in heaven it will not be
allowed.

252. Familiarity breeds contempt. How accurate that is. The reason we hold truth in such respect is because we have so little opportunity to get familiar with it.

253. If I cannot swear in heaven I shall not stay there.

254. The unspoken word is capital. We can invest it or we can squander it.

255. If you wish to lower yourself in a person's favor, one good way is to tell his story over again, the way *you* heard it.

256. Spending one's capital is feeding a dog on his own tail.

257. Good breeding consists in concealing how much we think of ourselves and how little we think of the other person.

258. Truth is more of a stranger than fiction.

259. There are no grades of vanity, there are only grades of ability in concealing it.

260. When we remember that we are all mad, the mysteries disappear and life stands explained.

261. It is not best that we use our morals week days; it gets them out of repair for Sundays.

262. Truth is mighty and will prevail. There is nothing the matter with this, except that it ain't so.

263. All people have had ill luck, but Jairus's daughter and Lazarus had the worst.

Like Lazarus, Jairus's daughter was restored from death; Luke 8: 41–56.

264. The human race consists of the damned and the ought-to-be damned.

265. When you fish for love, bait with your heart, not your brain.

266. The heart is the real Fountain of Youth. While that remains young the Waterbury of Time must stand still.

Cheap but accurate timepieces, "Waterbury watches" were so-called from their point of origin, Waterbury, Conn.

267. Christianity will doubtless survive in the earth ten centuries hence—stuffed and in a museum.

268. Shut the door. Not that it lets in the cold but that it lets out the cozyness.

269. It is an art apart. Saint Francis of Assisi said—"All saints can do miracles, but few of them can keep hotel."

270. It is easier for a cannibal to enter the Kingdom of Heaven through the eye of a rich man's needle than it is for any other foreigner to read the terrible German script.

271. Education consists mainly in what we have unlearned.

272. In this day of the telegraph man waits not for time or tide.

273. The altar cloth of one aeon is the doormat of the next.

274. "Good friends, good books and a sleepy conscience: this is the ideal life" (written in the Archduchess's album).

The Archduchess Maria Theresa entertained MT and his wife during their stay in Vienna, early 1898.

275. Concerning the difference between man and the jackass: some observers hold that there isn't any. But this wrongs the jackass.

276. Have a place for everything and keep the thing somewhere else. This is not advice, it is merely custom.

277.   There are many scapegoats for our blunders, but the most popular one is Providence.

1899

278.   [At a Boston lecture, arctic explorer Isaac Hayes] came on the platform, held his manuscript down, and began with a beautiful piece of oratory. He spoke something like this:

"When a lonely human being, a pigmy in the midst of the architecture of nature, stands solitary on those icy waters and looks abroad to the horizon and sees mighty castles and temples of eternal ice raising up their pinnacles tipped by the pencil of the departing sun—"

Here a man came across the platform and touched him on the shoulder, and said: "One minute." And then to the audience: "Is Mrs. John Smith in the house? Her husband has slipped on the ice and broken his leg."

And you could see the Mrs. John Smiths get up everywhere and drift out of the house, and it made great gaps everywhere. Then Doctor Hayes began again: "When a lonely man, a pigmy in the architecture—" The janitor came in again and shouted: "It is not Mrs. John Smith! It is Mrs. John Jones!"

Then all the Mrs. Joneses got up and left. Once more the speaker started, and was in the midst of the sentence when he was interrupted again, and the result was that the lecture was not delivered. But the lecturer interviewed the janitor afterward in a private room, and of the fragments of that janitor they took "twelve basketsful."

Speech at Whitefriars Club, London, 16 June 1899; *Speeches* (1923), 183–84.

279.   [Reflecting on how, in his youth, he had stolen a watermelon "out of a farmer's wagon while he was waiting on another customer" and the watermelon turned out to be unripe:] I said to myself: "What ought a boy to do who has stolen a green watermelon? What would George Washington do, the father of his country, the only American who could not tell a lie? What would he do? There is only one right, high, noble thing for any boy to do who has stolen a watermelon of that class; he must make restitution; he must restore that stolen property to its rightful owner." I said I would do it when I made that good resolution. I felt it to be a noble, uplifting obligation. I rose up spiritually stronger and refreshed. I carried that watermelon back—what was left of it—and restored it to the farmer, and made him give me a ripe one in its place.

Speech, New Vagabonds Club, London, 29 June 1899; Fatout, 331–32.

280.   I was always told that I was a sickly and precarious and tiresome and uncertain child, and lived mainly on allopathic medicines during the first seven years of my life. I asked my mother about this, in her old age—she was in her eighty-eighth year— and said: "I suppose that during all that time you were uneasy about me?"

"Yes, the whole time."

"Afraid I wouldn't live?"

After a reflective pause—ostensibly to think out the facts— "No—afraid you would."

Autobiography, ed. Paine, 1:108.

1900

The next four entries are from W. R. Hollister and Harry Norman, *Five Famous Missourians* (1900). The preface insists that the information, derived from "members of the families and personal friends of the subjects," is "authentic in all particulars."

281.   In November, 1839, [John Clemens] moved his family and household goods to Hannibal, then a prosperous river town. Shortly after their departure from Florida, some one, chancing to pass the house just vacated, heard a most vociferous wailing within. Dismounting from his horse, he pushed open the door, entered the house, and discovered Samuel sitting on the floor, his eyes swollen with weeping, and so frightened that he could not explain the distressing situation. With Samuel in his arms, the man

spurred his horse onward until he overtook the white-topped wag-
ons. When the mother, whose forgetfulness was occasioned by
assiduous attention to her sick baby, saw Samuel in the neighbor's arms, she made the remark, laconically, to her husband:
"Why, Mr. Clemens, we forgot Sammy."

P. 14.

282.   In personal appearance in boyhood, Mr. Clemens is described as having been a shaggy-headed, freckled-faced youth with
but one attractive feature — the bright eyes that twinkled from
beneath the heavy eyebrows. To add to this unattractive appearance, his early playmates tell of a drawling form of speech, which
has been characteristic of him in later years. Because of his eccentric disposition, many writers have said that Mr. Clemens af-
fected this peculiarity, but the following statement once made
by his mother disproves the assertion: "I-don't-know-what-makes-
Samuel-talk-that-way. Neither-his-father-nor-his-mother-talk-so-
slow-or-drawlingly."

P. 28.

283.   Sam Clemens' predilection for mischief and fun early
manifested itself. Among other similar stories one is told, an amusing episode that occurred at a candy-pull given by his sister Par-
melia [Pamela], who at that time was a music teacher in Hannibal. One night after the music lesson was over, the teacher and
pupils participated in an old-fashioned candy-pull. Samuel had
been early sent to bed as punishment for some offense, and was
not permitted to enjoy the festivities of the evening. After the
candy was made, the pans containing the confectionery were set
out to cool on the back porch adjoining Samuel's room. Immediately thereafter he was awakened by a cat-fight on the outside,
and the temptation to witness this rare treat was irresistible. So,
climbing out on the window-sill in order to better witness this
encounter, he lost his balance, falling down upon the pans and
creating such a rattling noise that the guests rushed out to ascer-

Cartoon courtesy of Watterson, copyright © 1983 by the *Mark Twain Journal.*

tain the cause of the commotion. They were some time in separating young Clemens from the sweet mixture.

P. 29. This of course is a version of MT's already famous tale of "Jim Wolfe and the Cats" which had appeared in the New York *Sunday Mercury,* 14 July 1867; rpt. Branch, *Literary Apprenticeship,* 268–70.

284.   At a New England society dinner Clemens had just finished a piquant address, when William M. Evarts arose with his hands in his pockets, as was his habit, and said: "Does it not seem unusual to this gathering that a professional humorist should really appear funny?" Clemens waited till the laughter occasioned by this sally had subsided, then arose, and, with his accustomed drawl, replied: "Does it not also appear strange to this assembly that a lawyer should have his hands in his own pockets?"

P. 76. The second half of this joke had appeared a decade earlier in Max O'Rell, *Jonathan and His Continent* (1889), 114–15. "Mark Twain is a man of quick repartee. A lawyer one day spoke to him with his hands in his pockets. 'Is it not a curious sight to see a lawyer with his hands in his *own* pockets?' remarked the humorist in his quiet drawl."

285.   [Discussing his servant George who bets on horses:] One night when I came home unawares, I found the house-door open. After going in and poking round, I rang up George. "Well," I said, "George, you've been here probably some hours with the house-door undone."— "Good heavens!" he cried, striking his forehead, and rushed up the stairs five steps at a time. When he came down I said, "Why, George, what was the matter?"— "The matter! why, that the house-door was left open, and that there were fifteen hundred dollars between my mattresses."

A.J.C. Hare, *Story of My Life* (1900), 6: 282.

286.   [A fellow passenger tells him he resembles MT:] He said, "Yes, you are a very good imitation, but when I come to look closer you are probably not that man." I said, "I will be frank with you. In my desire to look like that excellent character I have dressed for the character; I have been playing a part." He said, "That is all right, that is all right; you look very well on the out-side, but it comes to the inside you are probably not in it with the original."

Speech, New York, 17 Oct. 1900; Fatout, 346.

1901

287.   I remember on that occasion in the Hartford church the collection was being taken up. The appeal had so stirred me that I could hardly wait for the hat or plate to come my way. I had four hundred dollars in my pocket, and I was anxious to drop it in the plate and wanted to borrow more. But the plate was so long in coming my way that the fever-heat of beneficence was going down lower and lower—going down at the rate of a hundred dollars a minute. The plate was passed too late. When it finally came to me, my enthusiasm had gone down so much that

I kept my four hundred dollars — and stole a dime from the plate. So, you see, time sometimes leads to crime.

Speech to Jewish girls' school, 20 Jan. 1901; *Speeches* (1910), 102. Fatout prints a more dramatic version, dated 20 Jan. 1901, pp. 374–75. The basic joke inverts Franklin's anecdote of a similar event; Zall, *BF Laughing*, 54–55: "In the course of [George Whitefield's sermon] I perceived he intended to finish with a collection, and I silently resolved he should get nothing from me. I had in my pocket a handful of copper money, three or four silver dollars, and five pistoles in gold. As he proceeded I began to soften, and concluded to give the coppers. Another stroke of his oratory made me asham'd of that, and determined me to give the silver; and he finish'd so admirably, that I empty'd my pocket wholly into the collector's dish, gold and all."

288.   The girl who was rebuked for having borne an illegitimate child, excused herself by saying, "But it is such a *little* one."

"To My Missionary Critics," *NAR* 172 (Apr. 1901): 528. The germ of this jestbook favorite has been traced to the 13th century by John Wardroper, *Jest Upon Jest,* 162.

289.   Always do right. This will gratify some people, and astonish the rest.

Note to Young People's Society, Brooklyn, 16 Feb. 1901; *MTE,* frontispiece.

290.   At a time during my younger days my attention was attracted to a picture of a house which bore the inscription, "Christ Disputing with the Doctors."

I could attach no other meaning to it than that Christ was actually quarrelling with the doctors. So I asked an old slave, who was a sort of a herb doctor in a small way — unlicensed, of course what the meaning of the picture was. "What has he done?" I asked. And the colored man replied: "Humph, he ain't got no license."

Testimony before a legislative committee studying a bill to legalize osteopathy, Albany, New York, 27 Feb. 1901; *Speeches* (1910), 255.

The next four entries are from a speech before the St. Andrew's Society, New York, 30 Nov. 1901, where they illustrated the difference between conscious and unconscious humor; Fatout, 424.

291.   A man receives a telegram telling him that his mother-in-law is dead and asking, "Shall we embalm, bury, or cremate her?" He wired back, "If these fail, try dissection." Now, the unconscious humor of this was that he thought they'd try all of the three means suggested, anyway.

292.   Another instance of unconscious humor was of the Sunday school boy who defined a lie as "An abomination before the Lord and an ever present help in time of trouble." That may have been unconscious humor, but it looked more like hard, cold experience and knowledge of facts.

293.   Then you have the story of the two fashionable ladies talking before a sturdy old Irish washerwoman. One said to the other, "Where did you spend the summer?" "Oh, at Long Branch," was the reply. "But the Irish there; oh, the Irish! Where were you?" she asked her companion in turn. "At Saratoga; but the Irish there; oh, the Irish!" Then spoke up the old Irish woman, and asked, "Why didn't you go to Hades? You wouldn't have found any Irish there."

294.   Let me tell you now of a case of conscious humor. It was of William Cary, late of the *Century,* who died a few weeks ago, a man of the finest spirit and thought. One day a distinguished American called at the *Century* office. There was a new boy on duty as sentry. He gruffly gave the gentleman a seat and bade him wait. A short time after, Mr. Cary came along and said, "Why, what are you doing here?" After explanations Mr. Cary brought out three pictures, one of Washington, one of Lincoln, and one of Grant. "Now, young man," he said to the boy, "didn't you know that gentleman? Now, look at these pictures carefully, and if any of these gentlemen call show them right in."

1902

295. A man gets up and is filled to the eyes with happy emotions, but his tongue is tied; he has nothing to say; he is in the condition of Doctor [C.C.] Rice's friend who came home drunk and explained it to his wife, and his wife said to him, "John, when you have drunk all the whiskey you want, you ought to ask for sarsaparilla." He said, "Yes, but when I have drunk all the whiskey I want I can't say sarsaparilla."

Speech on his sixty-seventh birthday, Metropolitan Club, New York, 28 Nov. 1902; *MT's Birthday* (pvt. ptd., 1903), 41.

The next four entries are from *Two Hundred After Dinner Stories* (1902).

296. "When I was a youngster I attended school at a place where the use of the birch rod was not an unusual event. It was against the rules to mark the desks in any manner, the penalty being a fine of $5 or public chastisement.

"Happening to violate the rule on one occasion, I was offered the alternative. I told my father, and, as he seemed to think it would be too bad for me to be publicly punished, he gave me the $5. At that period of my existence $5 was a large sum, while a whipping was of little consequence, and so—" here Mr. Clemens reflectively knocked the ashes from his cigar—"well," he finally added, "that was how I earned my first $5."

P. 16. Marshall Wilder says MT told him the same story; *Wit and Humor of America* (1907–11), 1: 1.

297. At one of the public receptions at the White House during the second Cleveland Administration, Mr. Samuel Clemens (Mark Twain) was presented to Mrs. Cleveland. On shaking hands with her he gave her a card, asking simply: "Will you please sign that?"

Mrs. Cleveland glanced at the card to find nothing but the words: "He has not—" written across it. She looked in amused perplexity to Mr. Clemens for something further, when the latter explained: "My wife said if I came here I would be sure to come with my galoshes on; but I haven't, have I? So I wish you would sign that for me to give to her."

Mrs. Cleveland looked down at his feet and then laughingly wrote her name on the card.

P. 58.

298.   Mark Twain, relating several incidents of his travels in India, told the following story anent the pomposity of the Judge of the Bombay High Court:

"A Judge, whose bearing denoted that never for an instant could he forget his judicial distinction, was walking up and down the platform of a small railway station just before taking his seat in the train. A few minutes after the train had drawn into the station a perspiring Englishman rushed on to the platform and said to the Judge: 'Is this the Bombay train?'

"The Judge, looking over the head of the questioner, remarked coldly: 'I am not the Station Master.' Whereupon the Englishman retorted, with considerable heat: 'Then, confound you, Sir, why do you swagger about as if you were.'"

Pp. 113–14.

299.   Two Englishmen were discussing with Mark Twain the old topic of American humor as not appreciated by foreigners.

"But are the English really so obtuse?" asked one of them.

"Obtuse! You can't get an idea into an Englishman's head with a surgical operation," declared Mark Twain.

The questioner remained in solemn thought for a moment. Then he broke into a hearty laugh. "Quite a delicious joke!" he exclaimed. "Though, of course, if you were to open the Englishman's skull you would kill him, would you not!"

Mark Twain turned to the second Englishman. "What did I tell you? He wants to know whether it wouldn't kill him!"

The countenance of the second Englishman was like a blank wall. "Wouldn't it?" he queried.

P. 116.

The next twenty-two entries are notes dated 1902–1903 in *MT's Notebook*, ed. Paine, 379–85.

300.   One of the proofs of the immortality of the soul is that myriads have believed it. They also believed the world was flat.

301.   What is the difference between a taxidermist and a tax collector? The taxidermist takes only your skin.

302.   To create man was a fine and original idea; but to add the sheep was a tautology.

303.   None of us can be as great as God, but any of us can be as good.

304.   All gods are better than their conduct.

305.   Only he who has seen better days and lives to see better days again knows their full value.

306.   Circumstances make man, not man circumstances.

In Disraeli's novel *Vivian Grey* (1826), the "humorist" Beckendorff tells the hero the opposite: "Man is not the creature of circumstances. Circumstances are the creatures of men. We are free agents, and man is more powerful than matter" (1904 ed., 1: 608).

307.   Do not offer a compliment and ask a favor at the same time. A compliment that is charged for is not valuable.

308.   The man who is a pessimist before 48 knows too much; if he is an optimist after it, he knows too little.

309.   On the whole it is better to deserve honors and not have them than to have them and not deserve them.

310.   The human race consists of the dangerously insane and such as are not.

311. The time to begin writing an article is when you have finished it to your satisfaction. By that time you begin to clearly and logically perceive what it is that you really want to say.

312. We may not doubt that society in heaven consists mainly of undesirable persons.

313. Adam, man's benefactor — he gave him all he has ever received that was worth having — Death.

314. Martyrdom covers a multitude of sins.

315. Man was made at the end of the week's work, when God was tired.

316. Only one thing is impossible for God: to find any sense in any copyright law on the planet.

317. Whenever a copyright law is to be made or altered, then the idiots assemble.

318. There is no sadder sight than a young pessimist, except an old optimist.

319. When one reads Bibles, one is less surprised at what the Deity knows than at what he doesn't know.

320. It is not in the least likely that any life has ever been lived which was not a failure in the secret judgment of the person who lived it. It is not likely that there has ever been a civilized person 65 years old who would consent to live his life over again.

321. If man had created man he would be ashamed of his performance.

The following entries are from the pamphlet published privately in 1927 by Merle Johnson as *More Maxims of Mark*. Maxims duplicating those in earlier collections are not reprinted below.

322. All the talk used to be about doing people good, now it is about doing people.

P. 5.

323. At 50 a man can be an ass without being an optimist but not an optimist without being an ass.

Ibid.

324. Always acknowledge a fault frankly. This will throw those in authority off their guard and give you an opportunity to commit more.

Ibid.

325. Better a broken promise than none at all.

P. 6.

326. Benefit of Clergy: Half-rate on the railroad.

Ibid.

327. The burnt child shuns the fire until the next day.

Ibid.

328. Balloon: Thing to make meteoric observations and commit murder with.

Ibid. Since 1861, the U.S. Army had used balloons to direct artillery fire.

329. By and by when each nation has 20,000 battleships and 5,000,000 soldiers we shall all be safe and the wisdom of statesmanship will stand confirmed.

Ibid.

330. Do not put off till tomorrow what can be put off till day-after-tomorrow just as well.

P. 7.

331. Do not tell fish stories where the people know you; but particularly, don't tell them where they know the fish.

Ibid.

332. Etiquette requires us to admire the human race.

Ibid.

333. Everybody's private motto: It's better to be popular than right.

Ibid.

334. Every man is wholly honest to himself and to God, but not to anyone else.

Ibid.

335. Honesty: The best of all the lost arts.

P. 8.

336. Heroine: Girl who is perfectly charming to live with, in a book.

Ibid.

337. In literature imitations do not imitate.

Ibid.

338. It is best to read the weather forecast before we pray for rain.

Ibid.

339. It is a *solemn thought*: Dead, the noblest man's meat is inferior to pork.

P. 9.

340. Is a person's public and private opinion the same? It is thought there have been instances.

Ibid.

341. It is a wise child that knows its own father, and an unusual one that unreservedly approves of him.

Ibid.

342. The lack of money is the root of all evil.

P. 10.

343. The low level which commercial morality has reached in America is deplorable. We have humble God fearing Christian men among us who will stoop to do things for a million dollars that they ought not to be willing to do for less than 2 millions.

Ibid.

344. Morals consist of political morals, commercial morals, ecclesiastical morals, and morals.

Ibid.

345. Nothing is made in vain, but the fly came near it.

Ibid.

346. The New Political Gospel: Public office is private graft.

Ibid. President Cleveland's motto was "Public office is a public trust."

347. Never tell the truth to people who are not worthy of it.

P. 11.

348. None but an ass pays a compliment and asks a favor at the same time. There are many asses.

Ibid.

349. Nelson would have been afraid of ten thousand fleas, but a flea wouldn't be afraid of ten thousand Nelsons.

Ibid.

350. Optimist: Day-dreamer more elegantly spelled.

Ibid.

351.   Optimist: Person who travels on nothing from nowhere to happiness.

Ibid.

352.   An occultation of Venus is not half so difficult as an eclipse of the sun, but because it comes so seldom the world thinks it's a grand thing.

Ibid.

353.   Prophecy: Two bull's eyes out of a possible million.

P. 12.

354.   The real yellow peril: GOLD.

Ibid.

355.   Slang in a woman's mouth is not obscene, it only sounds so.

Ibid.

356.   Senator: Person who makes laws in Washington when not doing time.

Ibid.

357.   Taking the pledge will not make bad liquor good, but it will improve it.

P. 13.

358.   The trouble ain't that there is too many fools, but that the lightning ain't distributed right.

Ibid.

359.   We all live in the protection of certain cowardices which we call our principles.

P. 14.

360. What is human life? The first third a good time; the rest remembering about it.

Ibid.

361. Work and play are words used to describe the same thing under differing conditions.

Ibid.

362. We often feel sad in the presence of music without words; and often more than that in the presence of music without music.

Ibid.

363. You can straighten a worm, but the crook is in him and only waiting.

Ibid.

Professor Michael Temko reports that Merle Johnson added these maxims in 1935:

364. Clothes make the man. Naked people have little or no influence in society.

P. 6.

365. Let us save the tomorrows for work.

P. 10.

366. Vote: The only commodity that is peddleable without a license.

P. 13.

367. That George would refrain from telling the lie is not the remarkable feature, but that he could do it off-hand, that way.

Ibid.

368. [Recalling a dinner Andrew Carnegie gave for Sidney Lee, New York, 28 March 1903, MT] soared aloft in whimsical exag-

geration, casually dropping a reference to the time when he had
lent Carnegie a million dollars. Our smiling host promptly inter-
jected: "That had slipt my memory!" And Mark looked down on
him solemnly, and retorted, "Then, the next time, I'll take a re-
ceipt."

Brander Matthews, *Tocsin of Revolt* (1922), 272. Sidney Lee is said
to have recalled it differently, with MT saying, "I could let him have
the cash just as well as not, so I gave him a couple of million.—Do you
remember that, Andy?"
"No!" Carnegie answered vehemently; "I don't remember that at all!"
"That's just the point," MT continued, shaking his finger emphatically.
"I have never received one cent on that loan, interest or principal"; D.W.
Orcutt, *In Quest of the Perfect Book* (1926), 176.

1904

369.   Figures often beguile me, particularly when I have the
arranging of them myself; in which case the remark attributed
to Disraeli would often apply with justice and force: "There are
three kinds of lies: lies, damned lies, and statistics."

"Florence April 1904," *Autobiography,* 1: 246. In modern diction-
aries of quotations, MT is given as the authority for assigning this quo-
tation to Disraeli.

The next eleven entries are notes dated 1904 in *MT's Notebook,* ed.
Paine, 392–94.

370.   The only very marked difference between the average civilized man and the average savage is that the one is gilded and
the other painted.

371.   The critic's symbol should be the tumble-bug: he deposits
his egg in somebody else's dung, otherwise he could not hatch it.

372.   The course of free love never runs smooth. I suppose we
have all tried it.

The allusion is to *Midsummer-Night's Dream,* 1:i.134: "The course
of true love never did run smooth."

373.   An uneasy conscience is a hair in the mouth.

374.   God, so atrocious in the Old Testament, so attractive in the New—the Jekyl and Hyde of sacred romance.

R.L. Stevenson's *Strange Case of Dr. Jekyll and Mr. Hyde* had appeared in 1886.

375.   The skin of every human being contains a slave.

376.   There is nothing more awe-inspiring than a miracle except the credulity that can take it at par.

377.   In America—as elsewhere—free speech is confined to the dead.

378.   Whenever you find that you are on the side of the majority, it is time to reform—(or pause and reflect).

379.   Let us adopt geological time, then time being money,— there will be no more poverty.

380.   "Pop's down in the sty. You will know him from the hogs because he's got his hat on."

1905

381.   I have made it a rule never to smoke more than one cigar at a time.

Speech at his seventieth-birthday dinner, 5 Dec. 1905; Supplement, *Harper's Weekly* 49 (23 Dec. 1905): 1885.

382.   [George W. Cable reminisces about their visit to New Orleans:] Another of the things that I learned in that season twenty-one years ago, was that along with that perfect naturalness which was essentially his inherent character, Mark Twain on the platform practised a painstaking heart. Do you remember, my old

friend and big brother, that night in Buffalo when, after an ex-
cruciating succession of discharges of our shot, the steam-pipes
began snapping and snorting, and you dared not answer them
because you did not know how long they would keep up to the
last word, and you went on with your reading while on your tongue
all the time you had the request that "some one would please
ask the janitor not to grit his teeth so loud."

Harper's Weekly 49 (1905): 1889.

383. [A young fellow of twenty-three returned from a three-
year whaling voyage to find all his friends enrolled in a temperance club. After holding out for three weeks, he applied for
membership:]

And then he went away crying, and at earliest dawn the next
morning they came for him and routed him out, and they said
that new ship of his was ready to sail on a three years' voyage.
In a minute he was on board that ship and gone.

And he said—well, he was not out of sight of that town till
he began to repent, but he had made up his mind that he would
not take a drink, and so that whole voyage of three years was a
three years' agony to that man because he saw all the time the
mistake he had made.

He felt it all through; he had constant reminders of it, because
the crew would pass him with their grog, come out on the deck
and take it, and there was the torturous smell of it.

He went through the whole three years of suffering, and at
last coming into port it was snowy, it was cold, he was stamping
through the snow two feet deep on the deck longing to get home,
and there was his crew torturing him to the last minute with hot
grog, but at last he had his reward. He really did get to shore
at last, and jumped and ran and bought a jug and rushed to the
society's office, and said to the secretary:

"Take my name off your membership books, and do it right
away! I have got a three years' thirst on."

And the secretary said: "It is not necessary. You were blackballed!"

Speech at the Casino, New York, 18 Dec. 1905; *Speeches* (1910),
293–94.

1906

384.   The idea that no gentleman ever swears is all wrong; he can swear and still be a gentleman if he does it in a nice and benevolent and affectionate way. The historian, John Fiske, whom I knew well and loved, was a spotless and most noble and upright Christian gentleman, and yet he swore once. Not exactly that, maybe; still, he—— but I will tell you about it.

One day, when he was deeply immersed in his work, his wife came in, much moved and profoundly distressed, and said: "I am sorry to disturb you, John, but I must, for this is a serious matter, and needs to be attended to at once."

Then, lamenting, she brought a grave accusation against their little son. She said: "He has been saying his Aunt Mary is a fool and his Aunt Martha is a damned fool." Mr. Fiske reflected upon the matter a minute, then said: "Oh, well, it's about the distinction I should make between them myself."

Speech, Carnegie Hall, New York, 22 Jan. 1906; *Speeches* (1910), 112.

385.   One day when she [his mother] was not present Henry took sugar from her prized and precious old-English sugar-bowl, which was an heirloom in the family—and he managed to break the bowl. It was the first time I had ever had a chance to tell anything on him, and I was inexpressibly glad. I told him I was going to tell on him, but he was not disturbed. When my mother came in and saw the bowl lying on the floor in fragments, she was speechless for a minute. I allowed the silence to work; I judged it would increase the effect. I was waiting for her to ask, "Who did that?"—so that I could fetch out my news. But it was an error of calculation. When she got through with her silence she didn't ask anything about it—she merely gave me a crack on the skull with her thimble that I felt all the way down to my heels. Then I broke out with my injured innocence, expecting to make her very sorry that she had punished the wrong one. I expected her to do something remorseful and pathetic. I told her that I was not the one—it was Henry. But there was no upheaval. She said, without emotion: "It's all right. It isn't any matter. You deserve it for something you've done that I didn't know about; and if you haven't done it, why then you deserve it for something that you are going to do that I shan't hear about."

Autobiography, entry dated 12 Feb. 1906, 2: 93–94.

386. [Recollecting how the local newspaper celebrated a great local occasion twenty-five years earlier:] The little local paper threw itself into ecstasies of admiration and tried to do itself proud from beginning to end. It praised the orators, the militia, and all the bands that came from everywhere, and all this in honest country newspaper detail, but the writer ran out of adjectives toward the end. Having exhausted his whole magazine of praise and glorification, he found he still had one band left over. He had to say something about it, and he said: "The Essex band done the best it could."

Speech, Waldorf Astoria, New York, 29 Mar. 1906; *Speeches* (1910), 323.

387. Once, when I was an underpaid reporter in Virginia City, whenever I wished to play billiards I went out to look for an easy mark. One day a stranger came to town and opened a billiard parlor. I looked him over casually. When he proposed a game, I answered, "All right."

"Just knock the balls around a little so that I can get your gait," he said; and when I had done so, he remarked: "I will be perfectly fair with you. I'll play you left-handed." I felt hurt, for he was cross-eyed, freckled, and had red hair, and I determined to teach him a lesson. He won first shot, ran out, took my half-dollar, and all I got was the opportunity to chalk my cue.

"If you can play like that with your left hand," I said, "I'd like to see you play with your right."

"I can't," he said. "I'm left-handed."

Speech at billiard exhibition, New York, 24 Apr. 1906; *Speeches* (1910), 269.

388. I was scrambling along, earning the family's bread on magazine work at seven cents a word, compound words at single

rates, just as it is in the dark present. I was the property of a magazine, a seven-cent slave under a boiler iron contract. One day there
came a note from the editor requiring me to write ten pages on
this revolting text: "Considerations concerning the alleged subterranean holophotal extemporaneousness of the conchyliaceous
superimbrication of the ornithorhyncus, as foreshadowed by the
unintelligibility of its plesiosaurian anisodactylous aspects."

Ten pages of that. Each and every word a seventeen-jointed
vestibuled railroad train. Seven cents a word. I saw starvation staring the family in the face. I went to the editor, and I took a
stenographer along so as to have the interview down in black and
white, for no magazine editor can ever remember any part of a
business talk except the part that's got graft in it for him and
the magazine. I said, "Read that text, Jackson, and let it go on
the record; read it out loud." He read it: "Considerations concerning the alleged subterranean holophotal extemporaneousness
of the conchyliaceous superimbrication of the ornithorhyncus, as
foreshadowed by the unintelligibility of its plesiosaurian anisodactylous aspects."

I said, "You want ten pages of these rumbling, great long summer thunder peals, and you expect to get them at seven cents
a word?"

He said, "A word's a word, and seven cents is the contract;
what are you going to do about it?"

I said, "Jackson, this is cold-blooded oppression. What's an
average English word?"

He said, "Six letters."

I said, "Nothing of the kind; that's French, and includes the
spaces between the words; an average English word is four letters
and a half. By hard honest labor I've dug all the large words out
of my vocabulary and shaved it down until the average is three
letters and a half. . . . I am careful, I am economical of my time
and labor. For the family's sake I've got to be so. So I never write
'metropolis' for seven cents, because I can get the same money
for 'city.' I never write 'policeman,' because I can get the same
price for 'cop.' And so on and so on. I never write 'valetudinarian'
at all, for not even hunger and wretchedness can humble me to
the point where I will do a word like that for seven cents; I wouldn't

do it for fifteen. . . . I do not wish to work upon this scandalous
job by the piece. I want to be hired by the year." He coldly refused.

I said, "Then for the sake of the family, if you have no feeling
for me, you ought to at least allow me overtime on that word 'extemporaneousness.'" Again he coldly refused. I seldom say a harsh
word to anyone, but I was not master of myself then, and I spoke
right out and called him an anisodactylous plesiosaurian conchyliaceous ornithorhyncus, and rotten to the heart with holophotal subterranean extemporaneousness. God forgive me for that
wanton crime; he lived only two hours!

Speech, Associated Press banquet, New York, 19 Sept. 1906; Fatout,
523–24.

389.   [A.B. Paine's 1906 notes:] Early in December (1906) I accompanied Mark Twain on a copyright lobbying expedition to
Washington, an account of which is elsewhere set down and need
not be repeated here. Looking through the notes of that journey,
however, I find one or two that may be added, now.

We arrived in the evening and went to the New Willard, a
hotel boasting certain "latest improvements." For one thing, you
were sure of getting boiling water from the "Hot" faucet almost
instantly—it wasn't necessary to feel of it. Early next morning he
was in the bathroom. I heard the water turned into the tub, followed by a wild blast of profanity: "God-damn the God-damned
son-of-a-bitch that invented that faucet! I hope he'll roast in hell
for a million years!" It appeared that he had sampled the tem-
perature of the flow, as was his custom at home—ordinarily sing-
ing a little at such a moment.

MT's Notebook, ed. Paine (1935), 396.

390.   It was not much of a start for the day. When coffee came
up his tray was placed on a little table by his bed, which he had
got back into as soon as possible. The hot milk was in a good-
sized pitcher—of narrow-neck, wide-bottom design, something
the shape of a pear or a gourd. Seizing it with a jerk he slopped
an unnecessary amount of the contents into his coffee, and a good

deal into the tray. He banged down the pitcher and glared at it helplessly. "That hell-fired thing," he said, "one might as well try to pour milk out of a womb!" And a moment later, "I get so damned short of profanity at a time like this."

Ibid., 396–97.

391.   [Testifying on a copyright bill, 6 Dec. 1906:] I do seem to have an extraordinary interest in a whole lot of arts and things. The bill is full of those that I have nothing to do with. But that is in line with my generous, liberal nature. I can't help it. I feel toward those same people the same wide charity felt by the man who arrived at home at two o'clock in the morning from the club and was feeling so perfectly satisfied with life, so happy, and so comfortable, and there was his house weaving and weaving and weaving around. So he watched his chance, and by and by when the steps got in his neighborhood he made a jump and climbed up on the portico.

And the house went on weaving and weaving and weaving, but he watched the door, and when it came around his way he plunged through it. He got to the stairs, and when he went up on all fours the house was so unsteady that he could hardly reach the top step; his toe hitched on that step, and of course he crumpled all down and rolled all the way down the stairs, and fetched up at the bottom with his arm around the newel post, and he said, "God pity the poor sailors out at sea on a night like this!"

Fatout, 539.

392.   One day when I was in the garden, fifty feet from the house, somebody on the long distance wire who was publishing a story of mine, wanted to get the title.

Well, the title was the first sentence, "Tell him to go to hell." Before my daughter got it through the wire and through him there was a perfect eruption of profanity in that region. All New England seemed to be listening in, and each time my daughter repeated it she did so with rising emphasis. It was awful. I broke into a cold perspiration, and while the neighborhood rang with it, rushed in and implored her to desist. But she would have the last word, and it was "hell," sure enough, every time.

Interview, New York *Times,* 23 Dec. 1906, 1: 2.

1907

393. [Criticised for not speaking at dinner, he replied that the host had talked incessantly:] It reminds me of the man who was reproached by a friend, who said, "I think it a shame that you have not spoken to your wife for fifteen years. How do you explain it? How do you justify it?"

That poor man said, "I didn't want to interrupt her."

Autobiographical dictation, 13 Feb. 1907; *NAR* 184 (Mar. 1907): 569.

394. I know of a turkey hen that tried during several weeks to hatch out a porcelain egg, then the gobbler took the job and sat on that egg two entire summers and at last hatched it. He hatched out of it a doll's tea set of fourteen pieces, and all perfect except that the teapot had no spout, on account of the material running out.

"May 30, 1907," *MTE,* 23.

395. There was talk of that soaring and brilliant young statesman, Winston Churchill, son of Lord Randolph Churchill and nephew of a duke. I had met him at Sir Gilbert Parker's seven years before, when he was twenty-three years old, and had met him and introduced him to his lecture audience a year later in New York, when he had come over to tell of the lively experiences he had had as a war correspondent in the South African war, and in one or two wars on the Himalayan frontier of India.

Sir Gilbert Parker said, "Do you remember the dinner here seven years ago?"

"Yes," I said, "I remember it."

"Do you remember what Sir William Vernon Harcourt said about you?"

"No."

"Well, you didn't hear it. You and Churchill went up to the top floor to have a smoke and a talk, and Harcourt wondered what the result would be. He said that whichever of you got the floor first would keep it to the end, without a break; he believed that you, being old and experienced, would get it and that Churchill's lungs would have a half-hour's rest for the first time in five years. When you two came down, by and by, Sir William asked Churchill if he had had a good time, and he answered eagerly, 'Yes.' Then he asked you if you had had a good time. You hesitated, then said without eagerness, 'I have had a smoke.'"

Dated "June 1907" in *MTE*, 330–31. Churchill's own recollections of the event are in *My Early Life* (1930), 375–76: "He was now very old and snow-white, and combined with a noble air a most delightful style of conversation. Of course we argued about the [Boer] war. After some interchanges I found myself beaten back to the citadel 'My country right or wrong.' 'Ah,' said the old gentleman, 'When the poor country is fighting for its life, I agree. But this was not your case.' I think however I did not displease him; for he was good enough at my request to sign every one of the thirty volumes of his works for my benefit; and in the first volume he inscribed the following maxim intended, I dare say, to convey a gentle admonition: 'To do good is noble; to teach others to do good is nobler, and no trouble.'"

396.   [Concluding a curtain speech at the Children's Theater, New York, 14 Apr. 1907:] After he had told a story about a negro who had got a marriage license with the wrong woman's name in it, and had then decided to marry that woman rather than pay two dollars' difference "as there wasn't two dollars' difference between the two women," he left the stage and the curtain was lowered.

New York *Times*, 15 Apr. 1907, p. 9. He attributed the story to Kate Douglas Wiggin.

397.   Many and many a year ago I read an anecdote in [R.H.] Dana's book, *Two Years Before the Mast*. A frivolous little self-important captain of a coasting sloop in the dried apple and kitchen furniture trade was always hailing every vessel that came in sight, just to hear himself talk, and air his small grandeurs.

One day a majestic Indiaman came plowing by, with course on course of canvas towering into the sky, her decks and yards swarming with sailors; with macaws and monkeys and all manner of strange and romantic creatures populating her rigging; and thereto her freightage of precious spices lading the breeze with gracious and mysterious odors of the Orient. Of course, the little coaster captain hopped into the shrouds and squeaked out a hail: "Ship ahoy! what ship is that, and whence and whither?" In a deep and thunderous bass came the answer back through a speaking trumpet: "The *Begum of Bengal,* a hundred and twenty-three days out from Canton—homeward bound! What ship is that?" The little captain's vanity was all crushed out of him, and most humbly he squeaked back: "Only the *Mary Ann*—fourteen hours out from Boston, bound for Kittery Point with—with nothing to speak of!" The eloquent word "only" expressed the deeps of his stricken humbleness.

Speech, Lord Mayor's banquet, Liverpool, 10 July 1907; Fatout, 582. Ch. 35 of Dana's book tells about "a mean little captain in a mean little brig, in which he sailed from Liverpool to New York" whose vanity led him to "speak" "the Bashaw, from Canton, bound to Boston. Hundred and ten days out!" Asked in turn where he is from, the mean captain replies, "*Only* from Liverpool, *sir,*" and Dana comments; "But the humor will be felt by those only who know the ritual of hailing at sea. No one says 'sir,' and 'only' is wonderfully expressive"; 1869 ed., 413–14. This paragraph was inserted in Dana's revision of the book in 1869.

398.   I was to talk to a lot of Young Men's Christian Associations in the Majestic Theater on a Sunday afternoon. My secretary and I entered the place by the stage door and sat down in a box and looked out over a desert expanse of empty benches—wondering. My secretary presently went to the main entrance in the other street, to see what the matter was; just as she started the Young Christians came pouring in like a tidal wave; she plowed through the wave and by the time she reached the main door the place was full and the police, mounted and on foot, were struggling with a multitude of remaining Young Christians and keeping them back. The doors were being closed against the people. There was one last man, of course—there always is. He al-

most got his body into the closing door but was pushed back by
a big officer. He realized that his chance was gone. He was mute
for a moment while his feelings were rising in him, then he said:
"I have been a member of the Young Men's Christian Association
in good standing for seven years and never got any reward for it,
and here it is again—just my God damned luck!"

Dated 1 Nov. 1907, *MTE*, 6–7.

399. [Teasing Andrew Carnegie about his short stature:] Always when I see Carnegie I am reminded of a Hartford incident
of the long, long ago—a thing which had occurred in a law court
about a dozen years before I went there, in 1871, to take up my
residence. There was a little wee bit of a lawyer there by the name
of Clarke, who was famous for two things: his diminutiveness and
his persecuting sharpness in cross-questioning witnesses. It was
said that always when he got through with a witness there was
nothing left of that witness, nothing but a limp and defeated
and withered rag. Except once. Just that one time the witness
did not wither. The witness was a vast Irishwoman and she was
testifying in her own case. The charge was rape. She said she awoke
in the morning and found the accused lying beside her, and she
discovered that she had been outraged. The lawyer said, after
elaborately measuring her great figure impressively with his eye,
"Now, Madam, what an impossible miracle you are hoping to per-
suade this jury to believe! If one may take so preposterous a thing
as that seriously, you might even charge it upon me. Come now,
suppose you should wake up and find me lying beside you? What
would you think?"

She measured him critically and at her leisure, with a calm,
judicious eye, and said, "I'd think I'd had a miscarriage!"

Dated 2 Dec. 1907, perhaps as a draft for a speech at the Engineer's
Club, New York, 9 Dec. 1907; *MTE*, 44.

400. [Teasing Carnegie about his pet plan to simplify spelling:] Your simplified spelling is not destitute of virtue and value.
It has a certain degree of merit—but I must be just, I must be
sternly just, and I say to you this: your simplified spelling is well

enough, but like chastity—(artful pause of a moment or two, here, to let the word sink in and give the audience a chance to guess out where the resemblance lies)—it can be carried too far!

Reporting on his own speech at the dinner for Carnegie, 9 Dec. 1907: *MTE*, 60.

1908

401. Now, here is a gold-miner's compliment, and this one is forty-two years old. I remember the circumstances perfectly well. . . . It was in a log-house, a bare school-house, and the audience occupied benches without any back, and there were no ladies present, they didn't know me then; but all just miners with their breeches tucked into their boot-tops. And they wanted somebody to introduce me to them, and they pitched upon this miner, and he objected. He said he had never appeared in public, and had never done any work of this kind; but they said it didn't matter, and so he came on the stage with me and introduced me in this way. He said:

"I don't know anything about this man, anyway. I only know two things about him. One is, he has never been in jail; and the other is, I don't know why."

Speech, Lotus Club, New York, 11 Jan. 1908; *After Dinner Speeches at the Lotos Club* (1911), 348–49.

402. [A former employer recalls MT's turning up in Washington, D.C. "about the winter of 1867":] I was seated at my window one morning when a very disreputable-looking person slouched into the room. He was arrayed in a seedy suit, which hung upon his lean frame in bunches with no style worth mentioning. A sheaf of scraggy black hair leaked out of a battered old slouch hat, like stuffing from an ancient Colonial sofa, and an evil-smelling cigar butt, very much frazzled, protruded from the corner of his mouth. He had a very sinister appearance. He was a man I had known around the Nevada mining camps several years before, and his name was Samuel L. Clemens. . . .

"Senator," he said, "I've come to see you on important business. I am just back from the Holy Land."

"That is a mean thing to say of the Holy Land when it isn't here to defend itself," I replied, looking him over. "But maybe you didn't get all the *advantages*. You ought to go back and take a post-graduate course. Did you walk home?"

"I have a proposition," said Clemens, not at all ruffled. "There's millions in it. All I need is a little cash stake. I have been to the Holy Land with a party of innocent and estimable people who are fairly aching to be written up, and I think I could do the job neatly and with dispatch if I were not troubled with other — more — pressing — considerations. I've started the book already, and it is a wonder. I can vouch for it."

"Let me see the manuscript," I said. He pulled a dozen sheets or so from his pocket and handed them to me. I read what he had written, and saw that it was bully, so I continued, "I'll appoint you my clerk at the Senate, and you can live on the salary. There's a little hall bedroom across the way where you can sleep, and you can write your book in here. Help yourself to the whiskey and cigars, and wade in."

Reminiscences of Senator William M. Stewart (1908), 219–20, 222. Stewart dropped out of Yale in 1850 to seek gold in California, then became political boss of Nevada, its first senior senator, 1864–75, re-elected 1887–1905. He published his reminiscences when he was eighty-three and died, eighty-four, in 1909.

403.   All schools, all colleges, have two great functions: to confer, and to conceal valuable knowledge. The Theological knowledge which they conceal cannot justly be regarded as less valuable than that which they reveal. That is, if, when man is buying a basket of strawberries, it can profit him to know that the bottom half of it is rotten.

MT's Notebook, ed. Paine, 398. It is dated "Nov. 5, 1908," apparently his final notebook entry.

404.   I met Mr. [Horace] Greeley only once and then by accident. It was in 1871, in the (old) *Tribune* office. I climbed one or two flights of stairs and went to the wrong room. I was seeking Colonel John Hay and I really knew my way and only lost it by my carelessness. I rapped lightly on the door, pushed it open and stepped in. There sat Mr. Greeley, busy writing, with his back to me. I think his coat was off. But I knew who it was, anyway. It was not a pleasant situation, for he had the reputation of being pretty plain with strangers who interrupted his train of thought. The interview was brief. Before I could pull myself together and back out, he whirled around and glared at me through his great spectacles and said:

"Well, what in hell do *you* want!"

"I was looking for a gentlem—"

"Don't keep them in stock—clear out!"

MTE, 347–48. In a speech, 19 Feb. 1908, the story concludes with merely: "What in H—— do you want"; *Speeches* (1910), 173–74.

1909

405.   The first time [H.H. Rogers] crossed the Atlantic he had just made the first little strike in oil, and he was so young he did not like to ask questions. He did not like to appear ignorant. To this day he don't like to appear ignorant, but he can look as ignorant as anybody. On board the ship they were betting on the run of the ship, betting a couple of shillings, or half a crown, and they proposed that this youth from the oil regions should bet on the run of the ship. He did not like to ask what a half-crown was, and he didn't know; but rather than be ashamed of himself he did bet half a crown on the run of the ship, and in bed he could not sleep. He wondered if he could afford that outlay in case he lost. He kept wondering over it, and said to himself: "A king's crown must be worth $20,000, so half a crown would cost $10,000." He could not afford to bet away $10,000 on the run of the ship, so he went up to the stakeholder and gave him $150 to let him off.

Speech at Norfolk, Va., 3 Apr. 1909; *Speeches* (1910), 177–78. Even then a half-crown would have been worth about 25 cents.

406. [Addressing the graduating class of Miss Tewksbury's School near Baltimore, 9 June 1909:]

There are three things which come to my mind which I consider excellent advice:

First, girls, don't smoke — that is, don't smoke to excess. I am seventy-three and a half years old, and have been smoking seventy-three of them. But I never smoke to excess — that is, I smoke in moderation, only one cigar at a time.

Second, don't drink — that is, don't drink to excess.

Third, don't marry — I mean, to excess.

Speeches (1910), 107.

407. I remember when I had just written *Innocents Abroad* when I and my partner wanted to start a newspaper syndicate. We needed three dollars and did not know where to get it. While we were in a quandary I espied a valuable dog on the street. I picked up the canine and sold him to a man for three dollars. Afterward the owner of the dog came along and I got three dollars from him for telling where the dog was. So I went back and gave the three dollars to the man whom I sold it to, and lived honestly ever after.

Ibid.

1910

408. [Speaking as a publisher at the Author's Club:] He spoke of the multitude of young authors who beset every publisher and beseech him for advice after he has explained that their manuscripts are "not available" for publication by his own firm, with its peculiar limitations. Most publishers cruelly refuse, he said, to do anything for these innocents. "I never do that," he added. "I always give them good advice, and more than that, I always do something for them — *I give them notes of introduction to* [R.W.] *Gilder.*"

George Cary Eggleston, *Recollections of a Varied Life* (1910), 259. Gilder, editor of *Century* magazine, was probably in attendance.

The next five entries are from Alexander McD. Stoddardt, "Twaini-ana," *Independent* 68 (5 May 1910): 960–63. All are from 961–62.

409. At a recent public dinner he remarked: "An old saying of mine has been misquoted. I didn't say: 'When in doubt, tell the truth.' What I did say was: 'When you are in doubt, tell the truth.' When I am in doubt, I use more sagacity."

The dinner was 9 Mar. 1906.

410. Hartford did not know quite how to take the humorist. After listening to a sermon by Bishop Doane, then Doctor, Twain remarked: "I enjoyed your sermon this morning very much. I have a book at home which contains every word of it."

To the implied charge of plagiarism the Bishop protested.

Finally the lover of fun showed the clergyman an unabridged dictionary and said he "stood ready to prove it."

411. A friend once asked him about the cost of building his Redding residence. The architect's estimates, he said, had been so many thousands of dollars.

"Did it cost that much?" asked the friend.

"Well, half of it did," replied Mark Twain.

412. One Christmas Robert Collier wired that he was sending to the humorist to his Redding home, as a gift, a sacred elephant. The day before the arrival of the elephant a carload of hay was received, which Collier paid to have carted over to the Stormfield stables. For one whole day Mark Twain stormed against this freak-ish idea. Finally the pachyderm arrived. It was a handsomely carved imitation, two feet high.

413. To the reporters who met him in October 1900, when he came home from nine years' exile, having paid his debts, Mark Twain remarked: "Some people lie when they tell the truth; I tell the truth lying."

The next four entries are from "Stories of Mark Twain," perhaps by the editor C.D. Willard in the Los Angeles weekly *Pacific Outlook,* 30 Apr. 1910, p. 6.

414. A young lady who was introduced to Mark felt that it was her duty to talk about literary matters, so she asked him if he did not think that a book was the most useful present one could give. "Why, yes," he answered, half doubtfully. "Of course it depends in some degree on the book. A big leather covered volume is excellent to strop a razor on; these thin scientific treatises the French turn out are good to stick under a table with a broken caster; a large, flat atlas can be used to cover a window where the pane is broken; and a thick old-fashioned book with a clasp is the finest thing in the world to throw at a cat."

415. This is one his daughter tells. Mark was walking alone in London, when a well-dressed, pleasant-faced woman rushed up to him and grabbed both his hands. "I am so delighted to see you, face to face," she exclaimed. "I have always admired you so much." "Indeed!" said the proud author, elevating his chest a little. "Yes," continued the woman, "everybody here in England admires you. How proud America must be of you!" "And you recognized me"—began Mark. "By your pictures, of course. As soon as I set eyes on you, I said to myself: 'That's Buffalo Bill—the great Buffalo Bill!'"

416. Once when Mark was returning from Europe he was met by a reporter who told him that during his absence a dispatch had come from Missouri, announcing that the house in which he was born had burned up. "There it is again," said Mark gloomily, "usually when I am away it gets sold, and nobody ever gives me the money. This time it burns up, and I probably won't get a cent of the insurance."

417. When the author of "John Bull and His Island" wrote up his travels in America he said that the average American did not know who his grandfather was; to which Mark Twain made the famous retort that the American was, however, one degree better off than the Frenchman who, as a rule, was in considerable doubt as to who his father was.

The editor has confused his Frenchmen: the author of *John Bull and His Island* was Paul Blouët but the allusion is to Paul Bourget's *Outremer* (1895), which MT reviewed in *NAR* 160 (Jan. 1895): 48–62, commenting on French paternity on 62.

418. He confessed to me once that at gatherings when speech-making was expected, he preferred to do his part after others had done theirs, for what was said before made opportunities for him later on. An instance of this occurred at a breakfast in London given during his last visit to England. Augustine Birrell, the Irish secretary, preceded him, and referring to the demands made on him in what is probably the most irritating and laborious of all parliamentary offices, declared, "I am sure I don't know how I got here."

That gave Clemens the chance he had waited for. . . . "Mr. Birrell," he began very slowly and with a more expansive style than usual, "Mr. Birrell has just said he doesn't know how he got here." Then he bent over the Irish secretary, and looked into his wine glasses. "Doesn't know how he got here"—very significantly. Mr. Birrell was puzzled behind his spectacles, and everybody was on the *qui vive* just as the speaker liked to have them; it was a part of his game.

"Well, he hasn't—had—anything—" a prolonged pause. "Anything—more—to—drink—since he came, and we'll at least see that he gets home all right."

William H. Rideing, *Bookman* 31 (June 1910): 381–82.

419. One evening a few years ago Brander Matthews and Francis Wilson were dining together at the Players Club of New York, when the former made the suggestion that they write a letter to Mark Twain. "But," objected Mr. Wilson, "we don't know where he is," for it was at a time when Mr. Clemens was away ravelling somewhere. "Oh," said Professor Matthews, "that does not make any difference. It is sure to find him. I think he is some place in Europe so we had better put on a five-cent stamp." So the two sat down and composed a letter which they addressed to

MARK TWAIN,

GOD KNOWS WHERE

Within three weeks they received a reply from Mr. Clemens which said briefly: "He did."

Bookman 31 (July 1910): 458.

420. Upon the death of Lincoln many obituary poems sprang into print, among them one which took the fancy of Mark Twain, who set it off thus:

> Gone, gone, gone,
> Gone to his endeavor;
> Gone, gone, gone,
> Forever and forever.

"This is a very nice refrain to this little poem. But if there *is* any criticism to make upon it, I should say that there was a little too much 'gone' and not enough 'forever!'"

G.W. James, "MT and the Pacific Coast," *Pacific Monthly* 24 (Aug. 1910): 124.

1911

421. Mark Twain was taken by a friend to Whistler's studio, just as he was putting the finishing touches to one of his fantastic studies. Confident of the usual commendation, Whistler inquired his guest's opinion of the picture. Mark Twain assumed the air of a connoisseur, and approaching the picture remarked that it did very well, but—"he didn't care much for that cloud—"; and suiting the action to the word, appeared to be on the point of rubbing the cloud with his gloved finger. In genuine horror, Whistler exclaimed: "Don't touch it, the paint's wet!" "Oh, that's all right," replied Mark with his characteristic drawl: "these aren't my best gloves, anyhow!"

Archibald Henderson, *MT* (1911), 111–12.

422.   [Warning two young burglars who had stolen silverware from his new mansion, Stormfield:] Don't you see where you're drifting. They'll send you from here down to Bridgeport jail, and the next thing you know you'll be in the United States Senate. There's no future left open to you.

   Ibid., 114.

1912

423.   After the Corbett-Sullivan fight in New Orleans those pugilists gave an exhibition of their boxing prowess in the Madison Square Garden; and Mark Twain, being in the city at the time, asked me if I could secure him a good seat for the performance. We went to see the friendly sparring match; and after it was over, Clemens informed me that he should like to meet Corbett, so I took him into Corbett's dressing-room, where the athlete was having a rub-down after his encounter, and introduced him. Clemens, in his slow, drawling manner of speech, said: "I am pleased to meet you, Mr. Corbett. I am informed that you now propose to go over to London to make a match for the championship of the world." Corbett said that he had that idea in mind. "Now, before you do that," Clemens went on to say, "you must first put the gloves on with me." "That would hardly be fair," Corbett promptly replied, "for if you should get the best of me, I would be down and out; but if I succeeded in whipping you, you would still be Mark Twain." This was too much for Clemens, and we accordingly beat a hasty retreat.

   J. Henry Harper, *The House of Harper* (1912), 578–79.

424.   He told how at one time he was riding over the prairies in a wagon without springs, when the driver carelessly drove over a boulder and he was unceremoniously jolted out. When the driver came back to help him up he inquired if he was much hurt. Clemens replied no, but if he ever went to hell he would like to be taken there in his wagon, and when asked why, he answered, because he would be so glad to get there.

   Ibid., 579–80.

The next five entries are from Albert Bigelow Paine's authorized biography, *Mark Twain* (1912).

425. [A colleague from MT's river days recalls one of his stories:] Boys, I had great presence of mind once. It was at a fire. An old man leaned out of a four-story building calling for help. Everybody in the crowd below looked up, but nobody did anything. The ladders weren't long enough. Nobody had any presence of mind —nobody but me. I came to the rescue. I yelled for a rope. When it came I threw the old man the end of it. He caught it and I told him to tie it around his waist. He did so, and I pulled him down.

P. 149.

426. [A colleague from military service recalls an adventure:] The little mule refused to cross the river; so Ab Grimes took the coil of rope, hitched one end of it to his own saddle and the other end to Paint Brush's neck. Grimes was mounted on a big horse, and when he started it was necessary for Paint Brush to follow. Arriving at the farther bank, Grimes looked around, and was horrified to see that the end of the rope led down in the water with no horse and rider in view. He spurred up the bank, and the hat of Lieutenant Clemens and the ears of Paint Brush appeared.

"Ab," said Clemens, as he mopped his face, "do you know that little devil *waded* all the way across?"

P. 167.

427. [The Holy Land tour] was a trying journey, and after fierce days of desert hills the reaction might not always spare even the holiest memories. Jack was particularly sinful. When they learned the price for a boat on Galilee, and the deacons who had traveled nearly half around the world to sail on that sacred water were confounded by the charge, Jack said: "Well, Denny, do you wonder now that Christ walked?"

P. 337.

428. He used to tell how, for a long time, he concealed his profanity from [his wife]; how one morning, when he thought the door was shut between their bedroom and the bathroom, he was in there dressing and shaving, accompanying these trying things with language intended only for the strictest privacy; how presently, when he discovered a button off the shirt he intended to put on, he hurled it through the window into the yard with appropriate remarks, followed it with another shirt that was in the same condition, and added certain collars and neckties and bath-room requisites, decorating the shrubbery outside, where the people were going by to church; how in this extreme moment he heard a slight cough, and turned to find that the door was open! There was only one door to the bath-room, and he knew he had to pass her. He felt pale and sick, and sat down for a few moments to consider. He decided to assume that she was asleep, and to walk out and through the room, head up, as if he had nothing on his conscience. He attempted it, but without success. Half-way across the room he heard a voice suddenly repeat his last terrific remark. He turned to see her sitting up in bed, regarding him with a look as withering as she could find in her gentle soul. The humor of it struck him.

"Livy," he said, "did it sound like that?"

"Of course it did," she said, "only worse. I wanted you to hear just how it sounded."

"Livy," he said, "it would pain me to think that when I swear it sounds like that. You got the words right, Livy, but you don't know the tune."

P. 559.

429. [MT recalls an interview with U.S. Grant:] Grant remembered "Squibob" Derby (John Phoenix) at West Point very well. He said that Derby was always drawing caricatures of the professors and playing jokes on everybody. He told a thing which I had heard before but had never seen in print. A professor questioning a class concerning certain particulars of a possible siege said, "Suppose a thousand men are besieging a fortress whose equipment of provisions is so-and-so; it is a military axiom that at the end of forty-five days the fort will surrender. Now, young men, if any of you were in command of such a fortress, how would you proceed?"

Derby held up his hand in token that he had an answer for that question. He said, "I would march out, let the enemy in, and at the end of forty-five days I would change places with him."

Pp. 712–13. The story had appeared in print, in the *Squibob Papers* (1865); G.R. Stewart, *John Phoenix* (1937), 222.

1913

430.   Wells Fargo coach was robbed of $25,000 at the Mound House, half way between Virginia City and Carson. A week later some of the wild chaps in Virginia City held up Mark Twain on the divide between Virginia City and Gold Hill and took his watch and money. He thought it was a genuine hold-up, and decided to go the next evening to San Francisco for a brief vacation. As he was sitting in the coach in front of the International Hotel waiting for the hour of departure, the same gang, headed by George Birdsall, approached the stage and passed him a package done up in paper. He tore the paper open and saw inside his watch, and realized that his robbery was all a fake, and with his drawl said:

"It is all right, gentlemen, but you did it a damn sight too well for amateurs. Never mind this little dab of mine, but what did you do with the $25,000 that you took from Wells Fargo last week?"

C.C. Goodwin, *As I Remember Them* (1913), 255–56.

431.   He was in San Francisco when that city suffered a severe shock of earthquake. It happened one Sabbath morning about ten o'clock and Mark wrote a description of it to the *Enterprise*. The files of the *Enterprise* were burned and the letter, I believe, is lost to all the world: but some things about it seemed to me at the time about the jolliest writing that ever Mark Twain did.

I believe I can recall a few paragraphs of it from memory almost word for word. He said:

"When that earthquake came on Sunday morning last there was but one man in San Francisco that showed any presence of mind, and he was over in Oakland. He did just what I thought of doing, what I would have done had I had any opportunity— he went down out of his pulpit and embraced a woman. The news-papers said it was his wife. Maybe it was, but if it was it was a pity. It would have shown so much more presence of mind to have embraced some other gentleman's wife.

"A young man came down from the fifth story of a house on Stockton street, with no clothing on except a knitted undershirt, which came about as near concealing his person as the tin foil does a champagne bottle. Men shouted to him, little boys yelled at him and women besought him to take their sunbonnets, their aprons, their hoop skirts, anything in the world and cover him-self up and not stand there distracting people's attention from the earthquake. He looked all around and then he looked down at himself, and then he went upstairs. I am told he went up lively.

"Pete Hopkins was shaken off of Telegraph Hill, and on his way down landed on a three-story brick house (Hopkins weighed four hundred and thirty pounds), and the papers, always misrep-resenting things, ascribed the destruction of the house to the earthquake."

Ibid., 256.

432.   The incident took place shortly before Mr. Clemens's last visit to Italy, a trip which was undertaken on account of Mrs. Clemens's ill health. For this reason he had gone to great pains to obtain, through a friend in Florence, the lease of a villa which had been recommended to him. The family had all been con-gratulating themselves that the extensive and troublesome nego-tiations had finally been brought to a satisfactory conclusion, when one evening out of a clear sky came a cablegram, announcing that the other party in interest had thought better of his bargain and had refused to abide by the terms agreed upon. Mr. Clemens could hardly believe his ears when the cable was read, and after recovering from his astonishment and making sure that there was no error in the despatch, he gave rein to his anger.

"Damn 'em!" he said. "I wish—I wish—I wish li-i-ightning would stri-i-ike 'em."

"Oh, Father," said his daughter, "now really you don't mean that!"

"Well, no," drawled Mark—"no, I don't mean k-i-i-ill 'em; I only mean mai-ai-m 'em for li-i-ife."

John B. Quackenbos, "Mark Twain in an Emergency," *Century Magazine* 85 (Feb. 1913): 637.

1919

433. Mark Twain was not often a practical joker, but I have heard of an instance when he is said to have successfully worked a joke and incidentally brought together two good men. Ex-speaker Thomas B. Reed and Mark Twain were on a train approaching New York, and Reed asked his companion if he could direct him to some small, quiet hotel where he would not be bothered. "Why, surely, the Hotel Gilder is the place for you. "Hotel Gilder? and where is that?" "Just behind the Brevoort House on Clinton Place—very small, very quiet—doesn't take in everybody. Just ring the bell and tell them what you want; if there is any trouble, ask to see the proprietor, tell him who you are and that I sent you."

And so it happened. And when the "proprietor," Mr. Richard Watson Gilder, came downstairs and found out who the guest was who so persistently wanted a room in his house, and who had sent him, it is not unlikely that the laughter could have been heard as far as Mark Twain's home which was around the corner and a block up Fifth Avenue.

William W. Ellsworth, *A Golden Age of Authors* (1919), 228–29.

434. When his story "The Million-Pound Bank Note" was published in The Century, we got up some very good advertising on it, imitation English bank-notes, posters, etc. We were cheered by the following letter. . . . It is the most variegated and extrao-

dinary explosion of advertising I have encountered in my lifetime.
Yes, and the most ingenious and seductive and beguiling, too —
for it made me go and get the article and read it myself, it so
inflamed my curiosity to know what it was all about. When advertising can achieve that effect, it has struck the very summit, it
seems to me.

I haven't read the rest of my works, but would like to — so some
time I will get you to advertise them, too.

Ibid., 229–30. The MS is reproduced on 222.

1922

435. [Publisher B.H. Ticknor sends regrets that he could not
attend a proposed meeting, concluding: "God be with you, for
I cannot."] Twain returned the sheet, at the foot of which he had
inscribed the words:
Dear Ticknor:

He didn't come. It has been a great disappointment to the
whole family. Hereafter, appoint a party we can depend on.

Caroline Ticknor, *Glimpses of Authors* (1922), 145–46.

436. He thought he could play Chicago pool, and in the earlier nineties used to choose me for an adversary. I was younger
and a better player than he. One day, having beaten him one
game, I dared to be winning another. He swore at me for some
shot I had made, so I said over my shoulder:
"Don't be profane."

Simulating great anger (he was funniest when he pretended
gruffness) his mustache bristled, his eyes glared, his chest stuck
out, and he marched up to me, his cue banging on the floor to
emphasize each word:
"Young man, you do not even know what profanity is. Profanity, sir, is the unnecessary use of profane words and, applied
to you, no such use in unnecessary. Go on with your ———
——— game."

Edward Simmons, *From Seven to Seventy* (1922), 313.

437. Another time, coming [to New York] from Hartford with his daughter, he took a green car at the station. It was very crowded and they had to stand. Mr. Clemens protested at the conductor pushing them about and punching his daughter in the ribs as he collected the fares. Whereupon he said:

"Jesus Christ! Do you think you own this car?"

"*I* don't mind being called that," said the humorist, "but my daughter lives in Hartford and is not used to such language."

Ibid., 315.

The next eighteen entries are from Henry W. Fisher, *Abroad with MT and Eugene Field: Tales They Told to a Fellow Correspondent* (1922).

438. [MT concludes the story about a Russian Jew who claimed to have been chased by forty-seven wolves:]

"You probably were so frightened you saw double," suggested the magistrate.

"There were 12 at least," insisted Isaac.

"Won't half a dozen do?"

"As I live, there were seven."

"Now tell the truth, Isaac. There was one wolf—one is enough to frighten a little Israelite like you."

Isaac, glad of saving one out of 47, nodded.

"But maybe the creature wasn't a wolf at all!"

"No wolf!" cried Isaac, "what else could he be? Didn't he have four legs, and didn't he wag his tail?"

Pp. 27–28.

439. [Alluding to Kaiser Wilhelm's dressing up for a masked ball as Frederick the Great:] He reminded me of the little speech addressed by a Cossack Chief to Orloff, the lover of Catherine of Russia. Orloff visited the chief wearing a French court costume. The Cossack began to laugh.

"What is there to laugh at?" demanded Orloff in a rage.

"I laugh because you shaved your face to look young and put flour in your hair to look old—both things at the same time," replied the Barbarian.

P. 33.

440. [Alluding to former beauty Jenny Stubel recently abducted by an archduke:] She reminds me of old Field Marshal Prince de Ligne, making love to a very young girl and succeeding, or nearly succeeding, before he had time to reflect.

"A million," cried the Field Marshal, "if I was a lieutenant now."

P. 46.

441. [Returning to Vienna from Budapest, MT claims to have heard this story "at the archduke Joseph's country place":] A great landowner, after a business trip of several months, returned to Budapest, and was met at the station by his carriage and pair that was to take him to his estate in the country.

"Everything well at home?" he asked the coachman.

"Excellently well," replied the driver, cracking his whip.

After a while the Baron ventured another question:

"Why didn't you bring my dogs along?" he asked.

"Dogs are sick, your Excellency."

"My dogs sick? How did that happen?"

"Ate too much fried horse."

"Fried horse? Where did they get that?"

"Stable burned down."

"My stable burned down, cattle and all? Awful! What about the castle?"

"Oh, the castle is all right."

The Baron thought it over for a space of a mile, then said: "You are sure the castle was not hurt by the fire?"

"Sure, only the two wings burned down."

"But the family is safe?"

"Yes, the family is all right."

When the horses entered upon their tenth mile, the Baron resumed his examination: "Children all well?"

"All well and happy, except János and Maritzka, who were burned."

"Burned, oh Lord! And the Baroness, my wife?"

"Oh, she is better off than any of us. God has her in His holy keeping. She was burned to death. Yes, indeed, she died with her mother and in her arms."

Pp. 67–68. Lincoln used a concise version of this jestbook favorite; *AL Laughing,* 157.

442. [Speaking about wishing to die at home:] Remember my story about the body in the morgue? They couldn't make out whether the person was dead or merely shamming death, and so they put a bell-rope in the man's hand, and later, when the man awoke from his deathlike sleep and rang the bell, the watchers got so frightened they ran away, and, it being freezing cold, the man died a real death.

P. 94.

443. [After having been mistaken for Theodor Mommsen, the classical historian:] I feel indeed flattered because somebody thought that I have the whole Roman world, with Poppaea and Nero and Augustus and all the rest, under my hat, yet, when I come to think of it, there is some difference between us two. *My* children know their papa, and I know Susan, Clara, and Jean. But think what happened to Mommsen the other day. He was proceeding to a bus from his residence, when an unmannerly wind carried off his hat. A boy, playing in the street, picked it up and brought it to the great man. . . .

"Thank you," said Mommsen. "I never could have recovered the hat myself." He looked the boy over carefully, and added:

"And a nice little boy. Do you live in the neighborhood? Whose little boy are you?"

"Why," said the kid, "mamma says I am Professor Mommsen's little boy, but I never see him. He is always among the Romans writing in a book."

"Bless your heart, little man," said Mommsen. "To-night I will surely be home early; tell your mamma, and ask her to introduce you and the other children properly."

P. 101.

444. [O.W.] Holmes told me that in the late seventies of his long life, facts counted no longer with Emerson, for his memory was gone. At Longfellow's funeral, which preceded his own by a few months only, Emerson walked up to the coffin twice, probably forgetting the second time that he had already gazed upon his late friend's face. When he had taken his last farewell, he came back to his seat and said to the person nearest to him:

"That dead man was a sweet and beautiful soul, but I have completely forgotten his name."

P. 103. This echoes the famous passage in Moncure Conway, *Emerson at Home and Abroad* (1882), 382: "At the funeral of Longfellow, Emerson twice walked up to the coffin, and gazed intently upon the face of his dead friend. Then he turned to a friend and said, 'That gentleman was a sweet, beautiful soul, but I have entirely forgotten his name.'"

445. [Repeating a story told by Andrew Carnegie about a Scotchman "who was always trying to show off in kilties":] At night the boys put up at a rather dilapidated inn, neither clean nor promising other creature comforts. But the girl who waited on them, maid or scullion, was a dandy—blonde and blue-eyed, rosy-cheeked and sturdy of arm and leg.

As she flitted in and out of the room, bringing whiskey and water, cheese, bread and dried fish—that was all the bill of fare afforded—the travelers' eyes followed her, and when she left the room there was many a knowing wink. Douglas got jealous of the attention bestowed on Miriam.

"What is there to go daft over?" he demanded peevishly.

"Well," said they in chorus, "for one thing, she has better legs than you, Douglas."

Douglas hotly denied the imputation. There was an argument, and it was finally agreed that the two be measured. If Douglas lost, he must pay for the night's reckoning.

Accordingly, Douglas was put to the tape, and the girl also. Miriam had a few more inches of calf, but the Scotchman was undaunted. "Have you ever seen finer thighs than mine?" he boasted.

The lad who had been doing the measuring got flustered, but

the girl laughed: "Don't be afeerd, Laddie; the higher you go the bigger they grow. I'll be the winner."

Pp. 105–106.

446. "People wonder why I spend so much time abroad," said Mark Twain at a little luncheon party in Vienna, where young wine, fresh from the vat, circulated freely. "One of the reasons is that I have no doubles in foreign countries, while in the States I had notice served on me twice a month on the average that I look exactly like Mr. Cobbler Smith or Mr. Bricklayer Brown. I was told they had the very same warts, in the very same places, where I sport them—accuracy or imagination, which? The day before I left New York I got a letter of that sort and, having booked passage and nothing to fear, I made bold to answer it.

"'My dear Sir,' I wrote. 'I was so much impressed by the resemblance that I bear your face, feet, hands, mustache, eyelids, ears, hair, eyes, eyebrows, cheeks and other things, that I had the portrait of yourself you so kindly enclosed framed, and hereafter I shall use it in place of a mirror when I shave.'"

P. 115.

447. On another occasion Mark said: "I was born too late to help ease Lincoln's hours of worry. Ward Hill Lamon, whom we met in Berlin, told me more than once that Lincoln would have been a constant reader of my 'literature' if he had lived long enough to enjoy my books, and none knew Lincoln better than Lamon.

"And when my girls admonish me to behave in company, it always recalls the stories Lamon told me about old Abe's awkwardness.

"When Abe and he were riding circuit in Illinois, they carried their office in their hats, and Abe contracted the habit of pulling off his hat from the back so as not to spill any papers. That was all right on the circuit, but in the White House it looked undignified. So Mrs. Lincoln asked Lamon, a most courtly gentleman, to remonstrate with the President and teach him to take off his hat 'decently.' 'Decently' was the word she used, said Lamon. He continued:

"'I did my best during a night's smoker, Mr. Seward helping me, and the President proved a good enough scholar for any high-school of courtesy. Eight or ten times he took off his hat properly, without a reminder of any sort. Then, at the good-night, I tried him again. 'Let's do it in the right courtly fashion,' I said, doffing my chapeau like the Count of Monte Cristo.

"'Here goes,' said the President, reached his right hand back, and pulled off his stove-pipe in the old Illinois circuit style.'

"You see," concluded Mark, "it was no use trying to make a courtier of Lincoln. The same here."

Pp. 118–19.

448. "Read [Dr. Samuel] Johnson plentifully, I suppose," mocked Bram Stoker, famous as author, critic, barrister and Henry Irving's associate.

"Not guilty—never a written word of his," answered honest Mark. "I gauge Johnson's character by his talks with that sot Bozzy, whom foolish old Carlyle called the greatest biographer ever because, I suppose, Bozzy interviewed Johnson on such momentous questions as: 'What would you do, sir, if you were locked up in the Tower with a baby?'"

Well, what would *you* do," asked Bram.

"Throw it out of the window to a passing milkman, if it was weaned and if there was no cow around," said Mark.

P. 151.

449. During my stay in Stockholm some one read the following from one of my books (translated): "The solemn steadfastness of the deep made the ship roll sideways." Great laughter. "And she kicked up behind!" At that the house shook and rocked and quivered with merriment and my fame was firmly established in Sweden. If I had told the audience that "Her majesty's dress crept along the floor for three minutes (count 'em) after the queen had gone," they would have risen to a man and kissed me.

P. 176.

450. [Telling a "yarn on life in 'old Nevada'":] He rode several

miles behind a prairie schooner "because of a red petticoat flut-
tering in the breeze at the tail end."

"That is, I thought it was a petticoat, but when I caught up
with the wagon on that spent mud turtle of mine . . . I found
it was only a piece of burlap displayed for art's sake."

"Did I curse ART?" demanded Mark, looking around the circle.

P. 178.

451.   "I never was boss in my own house, but I like other men
to be the he-brute for fair. At Ottawa I recalled a hundred times
Lola Montez, the girl who started the revolution in Munich by
wearing the breeches at the Palace.

"'I am the master here,' shouted King Louis, during one of
their rows.

"'And I am the *mistress,* don't you forget that,' replied Lola."

P. 210. Born in Ireland, Maria Gilbert took the name Lola Montez
when at perhaps fourteen, deserted by her sailor husband, she took up
dancing and visited Spain. Thence she toured Europe as a Spanish dancer
to great acclaim. For two years she was mistress to Ludwig I of Bavaria
before coming to the United States in 1851 and San Francisco in 1853.

452.   [Comparing Berlin women and American women:] "They
say God made man in his effigy. I don't know about that, but
I'm quite sure that he put a lot of divinity into the American girl."

P. 212.

453.   "How much time do you suppose you have gained by writing '&' for 'and,' papa?" asked Jean one afternoon at tea.

"Not enough to waste it on answers to foolish questions," replied her father severely.

Then he gave her a dollar, kissed her and sent her away rejoicing.

"That little blackmailer," he said, "was impertinent only to make
me mad, knowing full well that later I would chastise myself for
being a brute—still with a dollar fine I got off cheap enough."

Pp. 218–19.

454.   "He was a King even in his undershirt and drawers."—

(A verse in one of Grillparzer's Tragedies—which caused the play to be put on the Index by the censor.) This amused Mark hugely. But he had no sympathy with the author, saying: "He ought to have put pajamas on the cuss."

P. 219.

455. A Hamburg dealer in curiosities offered to sell Clemens two of Bismarck's hairs for a hundred marks a hair. Mark asked his secretary to write back that, according to the most reliable statistics, Bismarck had rejoiced in the possession of three hairs only and of that trinity enough had been sold already to cover the pates of a whole row full of bald heads on a first night in Broadway, New York.

P. 219.

456. [A former colleague recalls meeting MT in the Sandwich Islands:] On my return to Honolulu I was astonished to find that "Mark Twain" had arrived a few days before. He was in San Francisco when I left holding the position of reporter on the *Call.*

"How in thunder, Mark," I asked him when we met, "does it happen that you have come here?"

"Well, you see," said Mark, in his peculiar drawl, "I waited for six months for you fellows to discharge me—for I knew you did not want me,—and getting tired of waiting, I discharged myself."

James J. Ayers, *Gold and Sunshine* (1922), 223. The more common version has the editor telling MT he is lazy and good for nothing. MT replies: "Well, you are pretty stupid: it took you six months to find out what I knew the day I came here"; C. Clemens, *MT Wit and Wisdom,* 98–99.

1923

457. The preliminary offering on that evening was the reading in very monotonous style of a lengthy poem in perhaps a hundred or a thousand stanzas of ten lines each, semi-historical, with a tropical background of the South Sea Islands. I was extremely

bored myself, but very curious as to its unexpected effect upon
Mark Twain in the opposite box to mine. He leaned out farther
and farther, fixing his eyes intently upon the speaker. "The poem
must be better than I think," I kept saying to myself, for Mark
Twain's eyes never left the poet's face.

When the affair was over, Mr. Clemens joined Mr. and Mrs.
Laurence Hutton and me for supper at the Huttons' house. I had
never spoken with him before. Just after we had settled ourselves
in the carriage, he asked with his inimitable drawl:

"Who—was—that man—that read—that—so-called—poem
about Methuselah's life in the Indian Ocean?"

"That was Mr. So and So," answered Mr. Hutton. "He is not
only a poet, but a literary agent."

"Well—he ought—to—go to—h——l!" drawled Mark Twain
venomously, and leaving the painful subject, began a general discussion. He explained afterwards, less profanely, that he kept his
eye fixed on the poet for fear that he should go to sleep and tumble over the railing of the box on to the stage. "'Livy'" (his lovely
wife Olivia) "always hates to have me do that!" he said. "She is
so conventional."

Kate Douglas Wiggin, *My Garden of Memory* (1923), 240–41.

458.   [At the luncheon honoring MT's degree from Oxford, 1907,
the Maharajah of Bikanir] asked me as an American and an author to present him to Mark Twain whose work he knew and
admired, and feeling somewhat like "Alice in Wonderland" I es-
corted the magnificent being through the quadrangle to Mark
Twain's side. Mark, "most amiable and charming sir," as the
Chancellor had called him in Latin, was in great form, the idol
of the crowd; his wonderful white hair glistening in the sun, and
the Oxford gown with its brilliant hood setting off his fine head
and face.

"I like the degree well enough," he confided with his usual
informality to the Maharajah; "but I'm crazy about the clothes!
I wish I could wear 'em all day and all night. Think of the gloomy
garb I have to walk the streets in at home, when my whole soul
cries out for gold braid, yellow and scarlet sashes, jewels and a

turban! If there's a dearth of Maharajahs any time in India, just cable me, sir, and I'll take the next train."

Ibid., 306–307.

1924

459.   Twain and the financier, H.H. Rogers, were fast friends. On a time they were in Bermuda together. In return for much courtesy, they gave a dinner at the Princess Hotel. It was a period of criticism of great wealth.

Said one of the 'Mudians to Twain: "Your friend Rogers is a good fellow. It's a pity his money is tainted."

"It's twice tainted," drawled Twain—"tain't yours, and tain't mine."

Francis Wilson's *Life of Himself* (1924), 299.

460.   Not many stories of Twain are better than that of his experience with the talkative barber. When he had finished shaving his customer, the barber ran his hand professionally across the chin and, poising the razor above his face, said:

"Shall I go over it again?"

"N-o-o," Mark replied slowly, "I've heard every d——d word!"

Ibid.

The next eight entries are from the "Mark Twain Number," *The Mentor* 12 (May 1924).

461.   [After overhearing his physician, Dr. C.C. Rice tutoring his son in spelling:] When the lesson was over and the boy had gladly left the room, Mr. Clemens said: "Doctor, you are a fine teacher, a God-given instructor, but may I tell you one thing: do you know I hate those fools who spell correctly? I once won a plated watch chain in a spelling contest, and I have never amounted to anything since."

P. 49.

462.   He told me the old yarn of the patient who obtained a prescription from a physician, and, after looking at the paper anxiously, asked how much the medicine would cost. "About two dollars," said the medicine man. "Well, Doctor, will you lend me the two?" The doctor was indignant because of the waste of his time, loss of fee, etc., but finally said: "Here are the two dollars —you need the remedy; but give me the prescription; I want to make an alteration." The patient watched the doctor as he used his pencil on the pad and asked, "What did you do to that prescription?" "I scratched out the nerve tonic," said the doctor, "you won't need that." Mr. Clemens observed: "I have always admired that man. That was a noble piece of graft—an easy way of getting two dollars. I have thought of trying the game on you, but have never seen the time when I thought you had two dollars.

Ibid.

463.   Even as a child Mark Twain gave glimpses of the first outcroppings of the original genius that would one day amaze and entertain the nations. At bedtime he would sit up in bed and tell astonishing tales of the day's adventures, tales that caused his listeners to wonder why the lightning was restrained so long. Friends of his mother asked her if she believed anything the child said.

"Oh, yes," she replied, "I know his average. I discount him ninety per cent. The rest is pure gold. Sammy is a well of truth, but you can't bring it all up in one bucket."

P. 56.

464.   Mark Twain was often subjected to the importunities of young and aspiring authors who sought his advice and, in some cases, asked him to read their manuscripts. One of these had accompanied his request with an inquiry as to the right diet for an author, asking Mark Twain if it was true, as Professor Agassiz had said, that fish was good brain food. Mark Twain replied as follows: "Yes, Agassiz does recommend authors to eat fish, because the phosphorus in it makes brain. So far you are correct. But I cannot help you to a decision about the amount you need to eat—at least, not with certainty. If the specimen composition you send is about your fair usual average, I should judge that perhaps a *couple of whales* would be all you would want for the present. Not the largest kind, but simply good, middling-sized whales."

Pp. 56–57.

465.   In England he was asked why he always carried a cheap cotton umbrella. He answered: "Because that's the only kind of umbrella that an Englishman won't steal."

P. 56.

466.   In the summer of 1889, Mark Twain and Rudyard Kipling first met. Kipling, who had just begun to make his name known, was touring the world, and during his trip through the United States he went to Elmira especially to see Mark Twain. The account of the little visit and interview is described by Mark Twain as follows:

"Kipling spent a couple of hours with me, and at the end of that time I had surprised him as much as he had surprised me —and the honors were easy. I believe that he knew more than any person I had met before, and I knew that he knew that I knew less than any person he had met before—though he did not say it, and I was not expecting that he would. . . . [*sic*] He is a most remarkable man—and I am the other one. Between us we cover all knowledge: he knows all that can be known, and I know the rest."

P. 57.

467.   In April, 1910, he came home from Bermuda in a dying condition, attended by his faithful Claude and Mr. Albert Bigelow Paine, his friend and biographer. In the face of suffering, and while drowsy with opiates and propped up with pillows to give him breathing space in his cabin on the ship, his sense of humor did not desert him. Once when the ship rolled, his hat fell from the hook and made a circuit of the cabin floor. Though his eyes were dim with pain, the essential whimsy in him seized on that trifling incident.

"Look," he said, "the ship is passing round the hat."

P. 58.

468. A year before his death, while delivering one of his talks on astronomy, he had said: "I came in with Halley's comet in 1835. It is coming again next year, and I expect to go out with it. It will be the greatest disappointment of my life if I don't go out with Halley's comet. The Almighty said, no doubt: 'Now here are these two unaccountable freaks; they came in together, they must go out together.'"

Ibid.; earlier in Paine, *MT* (1912), 1511.

1925

469. [Jane Clemens] was very funny at times, but her humor was often entirely unconscious. When she was visiting in Kentucky in her later years she heard two men behind her in the train arguing about Mark Twain's birthplace, one insisting that he had been born in Tennessee, the other that it was Kentucky. Mrs. Clemens said to the man who was traveling with her, "Tell them he was born in Florida, Missouri." The man complied but it did not settle the discussion, one of the disputants insisting, "I'm sure you're mistaken. He was born in Kentucky." It was too much for Jane Clemens. Without the slightest intention of being humorous she turned around and said, "I'm his mother. I ought to know. I was there!"

Doris and Samuel Webster, "Whitewashing Jane Clemens," *The Bookman* (New York) 61 (July 1925): 533–34.

470. Once, after writing to her son, she exclaimed in mild surprise, "See what I've done! I meant to say 'Kiss Susie for me' and I've written 'Kill Susie for me.' Oh well, Sam will know what I mean," and she sublimely let it go! The following answer came from Mark Twain before it even seemed possible that he had received the letter. "'Livy,' I said, 'it's a hard thing to ask of a loving father, but mother is getting old, and her slightest wish must be obeyed.' So we called in Downey [the coachman] and I held the child with the tears streaming down my face while he sawed her head off." Jane Clemens was outraged, not by the news that her granddaughter had been dispatched, but by the *method* employed, and she kept repeating indignantly, "Sawed her head off! *Sawed* her head off!"

Ibid., 534.

471.   Mark Twain delighted in teasing his mother. He once sent her a letter carefully sealed and marked "Personal and Confidential." Mrs. Clemens refused even to open the letter when anyone was around, so she retired to her room very much excited. She came down a few minutes later, her eyes burning with indignation. The letter was in Chinese.

Ibid., 534–35.

1928

472.   He remarked that he made a point of the finish of a tale. "I try to get a double snapper at the end," he said: "one to produce the effect I seek; the other to prolong it. I have thought of a story, and I don't know how to end it.

"A young man raised in the country goes to New York and engages in business. He has a real talent for business. He succeeds; his rise is rapid; his work absorbing. Busy years pass. He has never found time to return to his native heath or even to get married. His health suffers from the strain of prolonged, unbroken devotion to his tasks. His physician tells him that he must take a rest. Well, he begins to consider how he will practise the difficult art of resting. He thinks of the old beloved countryside and especially of Mary, the girl in whom he was interested as a boy. He had heard that she had never married. He wonders if it is because she was as fond of him as he had been of her. He decides that he will return to the scenes of his youth and try to find Mary. That is what he does. He takes a train and after a long ride of a day and a night he disembarks and drives ten miles into the country to the neighborhood that he knew and loved as a boy. He is made welcome at the home of his Cousin John. He learns that Mary is away on a visit. He tramps over the familiar trails; he fishes in the brook that he had fished in years before; he rides over the lonely country roads. One day, riding alone in a top-buggy on one of these roads, he comes out of a piece of woods, and down a hillside. There opposite the road is the old swimming-hole. Well, it's a hot and dusty day. The road is little traveled. He says to himself: 'Why shouldn't I stop the old horse here and go and take off my clothes and jump into the water and have a refreshing bath just as I used to do when I was a boy?'

"He hitches the horse to the fence; takes off his clothes and jumps into the water and swims around just as he had done in old times. He comes out and dries himself as he used to when he was a boy, flicking off the water with his hands. He puts on his undershirt and his overshirt and his collar and his necktie, and suddenly he hears a team coming.

"It is near, and he hasn't time to dress the lower part of himself. He jumps into the buggy and draws the lap-robe over his nakedness, having decided to finish dressing when the team had passed. Suddenly a wagon comes out of the woods and down the hillside, and in the wagon he sees Mary and some friends.

"'Hullo, Mary,' he shouts, and she calls back, 'Hullo, Bill.'

"The wagon stops. Mary wonders why Bill does not come over and greet her. In a moment she jumps out and goes to the buggy side. They shake hands. She looks good to him. The same bright eyes, wavy brown hair and cheerful manner of old.

"She looked up at him and said, 'Bill, where are you stopping?'

"He said, 'Over at my Cousin John's.'

"'Well, if you don't mind,' she said, 'I am going to get in and ride over with you.'

"Now, in heaven's name, I ask, what answer will he make her?" We laughed but he did not. He looked sad as if cast down by this difficult situation.

Irving Bacheller, *Coming Up the Road* (1928), 284–87. In the *New Yorker* 17 (27 Sept. 1941): 58–61, Stanley Walker says Bacheller told the story to Bob Davis of the *Sun* "the other day" with Henry Whipple as hero and Violet Musgrave as heroine. Bacheller said MT told him the story about 1893.

1929

The next five items are from the "Mark Twain Number" of the *Overland Monthly* 87 (Apr. 1929): 97–128.

473. [Thomas A. Edison writes to Cyril Clemens:] Mark Twain once came over to my laboratory with George Iles. He told a number of funny stories, some of which I recorded on the phonograph records. Unfortunately, these records were lost in the big fire which we had at this plant in 1914. When Mr. Twain and Mr. Iles were ready to go back to New York a rain storm came up, and as they opened the door a gust of rain blew in on them both. Said Twain to Iles, "I guess we are caged for awhile." Iles, noticing a carriage at the door, belonging to a visitor, suggested, "Let us take this carriage." "No," said Mark, "it is not ours." Iles replied, "That don't matter, let's take it any way." Twain, in his drawling way, said, "Business man's idea! business man's idea!"

P. 102.

474. [His cousin, J.R. Clemens, reminisces:] "Dr. Jim," said Mr. Clemens to me one day in his most solemn manner, "I have in a safe deposit box the manuscript of an unpublished work of mine which is the best thing by far I ever did and I give you the following excerpt as a sample of its quality. Being last summer in Germany in the company of a crowd of German research scholars I was fired by their example to do a little research of my own and the piece of work I attempted was to answer the question as to whether or no ants have intelligence. And to this end I first had made about a dozen little toy churches and labelled them 'Presbyterian,' 'Catholic,' 'Methodist' and so on. Then I rang a church bell and turned loose a crowd of ants I had caught. I found the ants paid no attention whatever to my churches. This was experiment No. 1. Experiment 2 consisted in placing a little honey, say in the Episcopal Church, and ringing the bell. Before its notes had ceased every last one of the ants had entered the portals of the Episcopal Church. Experiment 3 was the transferring of the honey to the Methodist Church and ringing for service. The former devout Episcopalians now went over in a body to the Methodist Church. In short, in whatever church I placed the honey, there I would find the ants before I had done ringing the church bell. From these experiments there could be but one deduction, viz: that ants have intelligence."

P. 105.

475. Another and more delicate experiment along the same lines was further described by Mr. Clemens as follows: "Catching a whole family of ants and establishing them in a smart little cottage by a thread of running water, spanned by a single straw for bridge, I first painted the back of the eldest son bright blue for purposes of identification and after making him drunk, I turned him loose. He was met as he was staggering over the bridge by the old folks, who forgave him and put him to bed. Again the experiment was repeated with like results. But the third time the dissipated son was caught on the bridge staggering home, his old man, losing all patience, caught him by the scruff of the neck and the slack of his pants and threw him headlong into the water."

Ibid.

476. Exhausted to the point of extinction by a very full day in Chicago, Mark boarded the night train for New York and retired to his berth at once for (as he fondly thought) a long night of blissful repose; but just as he was slipping over the border line between waking and sleeping he heard an old lady's voice wistfully soliloquizing and telling herself how thirsty she was with the regularity and persistence of the ticking of a clock. "Oh, I am so thirsty." At last, unable to bear the nuisance any longer, Mark got up in his night clothes and groped his way the length of the cold, dark car to where the drinking water was kept. Filling a glass he carried it back to the elderly victim of loquacity and thirst. This good deed done and a payment in heart felt thanks from the old lady duly pocketed, Mark got back into his berth and pulling the blankets up over his head and with a deep sigh of relief and content snuggled down to sleep. But just as the Sandman was bending over him a now all too familiar and accursed

voice began to exclaim and kept it up at minute intervals the rest
of the night, "Oh, I was so thirsty."

Pp. 105, 125.

477. [Cyril Clemens reports a visit to William Gillis, "the only
living person who was a friend of Mark Twain's while Mark Twain
was living in California in the early sixties" and now nearly eighty-
nine:] Gillis told us the story of the "Chapperal Quails," the two
sisters who lived with their parents not far from the cabin on Jackass Hill. One Sunday afternoon Sam Clemens and Bill Gillis took
the girls for a walk, and on their way back getting lost, did not
reach home until 11 o'clock. The girls' mother was very angry and
blamed it all upon Sam. She said: My girls often went out before
with Bill Gillis and were never late, until they went out today
with you. It is your fault.

Sam saw that his presence was no longer desired, and was casting one final despairing glance upon the room preparatory to
his departing, when his gaze lighted upon a banjo. Snatching
this up quickly he began to play such favorite airs as, "Fly Away,
Pretty Moth" and "Araly's Daughter." He sang so well—Sam had
an excellent bass voice—that before long the household was in
tears. Sam and Bill then arose to depart, but the mother said
that she couldn't let them go without a bit to eat. They heard
a chicken squawk in the kitchen and in about twenty minutes
the old lady came in with a large platter of fried chicken and a
plate of biscuits.

As they were going home Bill said to Sam: "Well, you saved
your bacon."

"Saved my bacon," Sam replied indignantly, "that was the best
fried chicken I have ever eaten in my life."

P. 127.

The next twenty-seven entries are from Cyril Clemens, ed., *Mark
Twain Anecdotes,* comprising results of the second annual contest by
the International Mark Twain Society of Webster Groves, Missouri,
not to be confused with the Mark Twain societies of New York or Chicago, the former led by Ida Benfey Judd, the latter by George Hiram
Brownell.

478. Mark Twain was visiting in Washington during the time that Mr. Melville Fuller was Chief Justice of the Supreme Court. A little girl saw him on the street and mistaking him for the Chief Justice, whom he resembled a little because of his luxuriant white hair and mustache, approached him eagerly and said, "Oh, Mr. Chief Justice Fuller, won't you write something for me in my autograph album?" "With pleasure!" Mark replied instantly. Taking the book she handed him he wrote, "It's glorious to be full but it's heavenly to be Fuller." Signing his name he walked away without further comment leaving her to discover later the treasure she had unknowingly secured.

John M. Dallam, Pennsylvania — pp. 3–4.

479. Mark Twain met a friend at the races one day in England after the meet. This friend came up to him and said, "I'm broke, I wish you would buy me a ticket back to London." "Well," Mark said, "I'm nearly broke myself but I will tell you what I'll do. You can hide under my seat and I'll hide you with my legs." The friend agreed to this. Then Mark Twain went down to the ticket office and bought two tickets. When the train pulled out his friend was safely under the seat. As is usual, about half way the inspector came round for the tickets. Mark Twain gave him two. The inspector said, "Where is the other one?" Tapping his head and saying in a loud voice, "That is my friend's ticket! He is a little eccentric and likes to ride under the seat."

James Hood, Vancouver — p. 4.

480. Mark Twain and Chauncey M. Depew once went abroad on the same ship. When the ship was a few days out they were both invited to dinner. Speech-making time came. Mark Twain had the first chance. He spoke twenty minutes and made a great hit. Then it was Mr. Depew's turn.

"Mr. Toastmaster and Ladies and Gentlemen," said the famous raconteur as he arose, "before this dinner, Mark Twain and I made an agreement to trade speeches. He has just delivered my speech, and I thank you for the pleasant manner in which you received it. I regret to say that I have lost the notes of his speech and cannot remember anything he has to say." Then he sat down. There was much laughter.

Next day an Englishman who had been in the party, came across Mark Twain in the smoking room. "Mr. Clemens," he said, "I consider you were much imposed upon last night. I have always heard that Mr. Depew is a clever man, but really, that speech of his you made last night struck me as being the most infernal rot."

Emily W. Kemp, California — pp. 7–8. In Max O'Rell, *Jonathan and His Continent* (1889), 110–11, the same story is told about Depew and Horace Porter, not MT.

481. [After addressing a grammar school graduation, MT awards honors:] One of the boys of the class, a little fellow, had won a prize — a big Webster's Dictionary, and when Twain presented it he said: "This is a very interesting and useful book, my son. I have studied it often but I never could discover the plot."

Sydney Ford — p. 8.

482. Mark Twain — losing a clipping, got up and he began to explore the bed. It was an enormously large bed, and he began to disparage the size of it. "One could lose a dog in this bed," he declared.

Edwin Pickett, Arkansas — p. 10.

483. [H.H. Rogers had invited managers and staff from his firm to view the international yacht races from his own yacht. The races were called off because of foul weather.] As we were coming up the bay, Mark Twain was seated on deck surrounded by most of the company, when Mr. Rogers appeared and expressed his regret at our disappointment. Mark replied in his inimitable Southern drawl: "That's all right, Henry; it reminds me of a story. A farmer had fattened a drove of hogs and took them down to the local dealer, driving them along the dusty road in the hot sun. They couldn't agree on price and the farmer decided to try his luck in the next town about five miles away. When he arrived that afternoon, he found that he couldn't get as good an offer as in his home town so he drove them back again. On entering the village, he was met by the local dealer who started to josh him. The farmer listened for a few minutes and then answered: "That's all right, Zeb; it hasn't been such a bad day. I've had the company of the hogs both goin' and comin'."

William B. Dickson, New Jersey—p. 10.

484. Mr. Clemens was a frequent visitor to the Players Club and maintained a locker in the Club where he kept hanging an unused but good long tailed black coat, such as was in vogue in those days. A young man named Smith, also a member of the Club, knew of the coat, and one day said to Mr. Clemens: "Mr. Clemens, I have got to go to a funeral this evening and have no suitable coat for the occasion. You and I are about the same size. Would you mind lending me that coat in your locker?"

"Yes," said Mr. Clemens, "But please take good care of the contents of the pockets." Then Mr. Clemens went on his way.

When Smith took the coat he found the tail pockets partially filled with scraps of tin, tacks, nails and a miscellaneous assortment of such junk. He dumped the whole into a newspaper, handed it to the clerk at the desk, with instructions to keep it for the famous humorist.

The clerk made a neat package of this junk, tied it up nicely and wrote Mr. Clemens' name on it.

This happened several days before Christmas. That evening Mr. Clemens came into the Club accompanied by a few friends. The clerk handed him his mail and the package at the same time. The famous humorist began to exclaim to his friends about his popularity in getting a Christmas present so well in advance of the holiday. While he was talking in his well known vein he was unwrapping the parcel, and during his discourse the contents began to spill out on the desk.

Realizing instantly the origin of his "present" Mr. Clemens dryly said: "I hope that damn Smith's funeral will be a failure."

W.H. Wills, Minnesota—pp. 11–12.

485.   His reply to his hostess who asked him if he did not sing: "Those who have heard me say I don't."

Mrs. M. Maltby, North Vancouver—p. 12.

486.   September 21, 1909, I visited Mark Twain at his beautiful new house called "Stormfield" near Redding, Connecticut, in order to take part the next day in a concert to be given in his drawing-room for the benefit of a library he had recently founded in the village.

The affair was carried through with Miss Clara Clemens, the distinguished author's daughter, and Oggie Gabrilowitsch, the pianist, to whom she became engaged to be married that day. . . .

Every room on the ground floor of the spacious house was filled to the last inch that afternoon by a crowd that spread up the stairways, on the balcony, out into the pergola, everywhere indeed from which the music could be heard, even if we performers could not be seen.

We were introduced by Mark Twain himself clad in his distinctive suit of white flannel, which seemed to set off his magnificent head of snowy white hair, and he was in great fettle. After a little speech which convulsed his hearers, he presented us who were to make music for his guests, saying shrewd and complimentary things about each one of us men and in conclusion: "While Mr. Gabrilowitsch and Mr. Bispham are much better known than my daughter, they are not near so good looking."

Francis C. Iredell, Massachusetts—pp. 12–13.

487.   "While I was with the Morning Journal, Mark Twain visited Hannibal and delivered an address to the graduates of the high school," Mr. Brown said. "Late that night a message came from the editor of the St. Louis Republic to ask Mark Twain for his views on a certain subject.

"I took the message and went around to the hotel. It was not far from midnight, but the clerk obligingly showed me to the room of his distinguished guest.

"Mark Twain was sitting up in bed reading, and had a lighted cigar in his mouth.

"I showed him the telegram, which he carefully read, but said he could not answer the editor's question because of his literary contract; he could not give out any information on that subject.

"'Then I won't have anything to write about,' I said, badly disappointed.

"Mr. Clemens smiled. 'Young man,' he said, 'I've been in that fix many and many a time. Now, if I were the reporter and you were the man in bed I'd tell how, over the vigorous remonstrances of the clerk I'd come up here in the dead hour of the night and aroused you from a sound sleep to ———'

"'But see here, Mr. Clemens,' I protested, 'you were not aroused from a sound sleep. You were in bed reading and smoking a cigar.'

"The famous man sighed hopelessly, 'If you're going to let a little thing like that stand in the way,' he said, 'I'm afraid I can't help you. Good night.'

"As I was walking back to the office I thought over the matter and decided to send the story just as I have given it here. They ran it under a big head."

Edgar White, Missouri—p. 13.

488.   During his visit in Budapest, Mark Twain was feted by all sections of society. A particularly elaborate affair was a banquet given by the Lipotvarosi Casion (The Lipotvaros Club). During the banquet the first speaker paid a glowing tribute to the illustrious guest. He made a fiery speech, accompanied by gestures characteristic of Hungarian orators. The words rolled magnificently over the speaker's lips, and frequent applause interrupted the speech. At the end of the toast the glasses clinked. Fiery Tokay was drunk to the health of the great American. When the tumultuous applause had died down the toastmaster called on Mark Twain. Deafening applause greeted the guest of honor, and it took several minutes before he could start his response to the toast. In deepest silence, with every ear strained in attention, Mark Twain said:

"I am deeply moved by the generous tribute paid to me by your speaker. I enjoyed his speech and only wish I knew your beautiful language so that I could have followed what your speaker

said literally, and not merely by intuition. I enjoyed the beautiful sound of your sonorous language—"

Startled by some strange expression breaking out on the faces
of his hearers, Mark Twain stopped for a moment. The toastmaster got up, bowed respectfully to Mark Twain, and said: "But sir,
Mr. X has given his toast in English."

Rosika Schwimmer, New York City—pp. 13–14.

489.   In a minor tournament of horse-billiards Mark Twain won
the prize, a Waterbury watch. Nine months later when he was
in Pretoria, South Africa, he had occasion to use the watch which
he had put away in his trunk. He took the watch out and set it
by the great clock in the Parliament House. He was unaware that
this clock strikes the succeeding hour every half hour, and when
the Parliament clock struck ten his watch, which showed the correct time, showed only 9:30. He shoved it half an hour ahead,
and at ten the Parliament clock struck ten again. His watch showed
10:30. He set it back again. At 10:30 the Parliament clock struck
11 and his watch showed 10:30. He pushed his watch ahead again
with some show of temper. In half an hour the Parliament clock
struck 11 again, and he found that the watch showed 11:30. "And,"
he said when later relating this incident, "I beat her brains out.
I was sorry next day when I found out."

P. 14.

490.   It was said that Mark Twain received a dollar a word for
his writings. Accordingly, a wag enclosed one dollar in a note which
he wrote to the great humorist, saying, "Please send me a word."

The written reply, which came promptly, contained one word
—the word "Thanks."

Florence B. Hatch, Washington—p. 15. Coincidentally, G.B. Shaw
inscribed a copy of *Cashel Byron's Profession* to an American who sent
him a dollar. Shaw said if every American autograph collector would
do the same, "I should be a millionaire"; Archibald Henderson, *Bernard Shaw, Playboy and Prophet* (1932), 700.

491.   About the New Year of 1891 the New York Sun of those
days published a squib referring to Mark Twain. In it Twain was

quoted as "wishing everyone a Happy New Year except the inventor of the telephone." . . . In an effort to learn what was amiss, the local representative of the company in Hartford was despatched post-haste to interview Mr. Clemens and learn the reason for his dissatisfaction with the telephone and its inventor. Mr. Clemens explained —

"I had no intention of reflecting on the inventor of the telephone when I started to write. I intended to wish everyone a Happy New Year, with the exception of the Emperor of Russia, and I had gotten the matter written up and upon reading it over thought the last part was not quiet enough and so I doctored it up a little, and then the first part was not satisfactory. Just then the telephone rang, and Mrs. Clemens said to me, 'Samuel you had better wait until John comes in and let him answer the telephone because you always lose your temper.' But John didn't come in, and I went to the telephone and, as usual, lost my temper, but couldn't say anything because the house was full of company, so I hung up the telephone in disgust and went back to my writing, and instead of the Emperor of Russia I put in the inventor of the telephone."

Parker Lewis, Connecticut — p. 15.

492.　Upon arriving at a hotel in a Canadian city, the humorist, glancing at the list of earlier registrations, took note of the one preceding his own, "Baroness X—— and suite." The hotel clerk reading the inscription, found the last arrival to be — "Mark Twain — and valise."

Maud Augusta Evans, Massachusetts — p. 15. In his collection of 1935, *Wit and Wisdom of MT,* Cyril Clemens repeated this version but in his *MT Jest Book* of 1963, he recycled it: "When Richard Harding Davis signed as 'Richard Harding Davis and Valet,' Mark Twain wrote: 'Mark Twain and Valise'" (20).

493.　During a sojourn in London, Mark Twain was a guest at a banquet of English scholars. The conversation drifted into a discussion of the Bacon-Shakespeare controversy. The party became divided in its opinion, and finally one desperate person turned to Mark Twain, who had not entered the discussion, and begged him to commit himself. Mark Twain replied, "I'll wait until I get to Heaven and ask Shakespeare who did write his plays."

"I don't think, Mr. Clemens, that you will find Shakespeare in Heaven," replied the loyal Baconite. "Then," replied Mark Twain, "You ask him."

Catherine S. Mubley, Massachusetts — p. 17.

494. Mark Twain for many years made his home in Hartford, Connecticut. He made there many friends; prominent among them was Rev. Joseph Twichell. When at his home in Hartford Mr. Clemens attended Mr. Twichell's church. One Sunday he became intensely interested in the sermon, and listened with unusual attention. At the close of the service, he approached his preacher-friend and in his inimitable drawl greeted him: "Joe, this mustn't happen again. When I go to church, I go for a good rest and quiet nap. Today I haven't been able to get a single wink. I tell you it won't do; and it must not happen again."

Elizabeth W. Cleaveland, Connecticut — pp. 17–18.

495. [As a young reporter on the San Francisco *Call,* he took up the study of French and took to eating weekly at a French cafe:] One day, as he and his roommate were coming out of the cafe, they found on the sidewalk, just outside the door a Frenchman. He was asking first one passerby and then another the way to a certain street, but no one understood him. That was Mark's chance. The Frenchman looked at him with wistful eyes and began to talk. Mark listened attentively. Three or four times the Frenchman was compelled to repeat the question; then Mark seemed to catch the first of the inquiry. But he had scarcely spoken half a dozen words in reply when the Frenchman fell to the sidewalk in a dead faint.

The true cause of the stranger's fainting never became known. Very likely he was famished, and perhaps he had been put out of this very restaurant because of his seedy appearance. But whatever the cause, the joke was on Mark. For once Mark's roommate was careful enough of his friendship not to tell the incident at the office of the Call, but teased the rising humorist a good deal about it. When the fun had lasted long enough Mark set his jaw,

and with unlimited determination written on his features announced: "I'll learn French if it kills every Frenchman in the
country."

Mrs. John H. McClure, Massachusetts—pp. 18–19.

496. In a set of Mark Twain we find a letter of Mark's tipped
in, which says: "I can't do no literary work the rest of this year
because I'm meditating another lawsuit and looking around for
a defendant."

G. Lawrence, New York City—p. 19.

497. In order to get material for an advertisement of a new serial
by Mark Twain which the Century Magazine was about to publish I went one morning to Mr. Gilder's room (Richard Watson
Gilder was then editor of the magazine) to look over the galley
proofs of the first chapters of "Pudd'nhead Wilson." It was early
in the morning and none of the editors had as yet arrived, but
seated in Mr. Gilder's chair with a pipe in his mouth and his feet
on the desk was Mark Twain, making pencil corrections on the
proofs I wanted.

It should be said here that Mark Twain had a system of punctuation of his own, while the magazine had its own rules regarding punctuation which the printers (the DeVinne Press) had naturally followed in setting "Pudd'nhead Wilson"; about the time
I entered the room it must have dawned on Mr. Clemens that
the corrections he was making in the proof were not merely typo-
graphical errors, but that his punctuation had been purposely
altered.

Glancing at me from under his bushy brows he said in that
drawling voice of his: "In the beginning God Almighty made men,
and then He made damn fools, and when He got His hand in
He must have made printers."

Charles L. Benjamin, Chicago—p. 20.

498. Woodland Street, Hartford, was a beautiful macadamed
residential street in the days when the high wheel was on the de-
cline and the safety bicycle with hard tires was just coming into

popularity. Our gas connection with the street main had sprung a leak, and it had been necessary to dig up the street to find this trouble, which having been cared for and the trench filled in, left one of those long unsightly as well as uncomfortable hummocks, well beyond the center of the road, as is always the case when macadam road beds are interfered with. One good sized stone, about the size of a cantaloupe, had been dislodged and gotten into the middle of that part of the street not dug up.

With this stage setting, let us go back a few days and say that "Uncle Mark" had been receiving lessons in bicycle riding for several days, up and down the Twichell driveway, and had progressed to the point where the Reverend Joseph Twichell (who was an accomplished artist on the bike) suggested that they take a ride for a few blocks on this beautiful summer evening; and they set out, down the driveway, turned into the street, and headed to pass our house.

The Reverend Joe was talking, advising and encouraging. "Uncle Mark" was attending strictly to business, saying nothing, and maybe grumbling a little to himself as he felt his responsibility. All went well, and progress of events was being watched by our family from our verandah, while several of the Twichells were a couple of hundred feet away at the end of their driveway. Both "Uncle Mark" and the Reverend had lusty voices, and they never whispered.

The advice and encouragement of Reverend Twichell were very clear to all. He started to go to one side of the street to avoid that macadam lump, and advised "Uncle Mark" of the whys and wherefores of his action. All was bliss for the novice up to this point, but everyone who has learned to ride a wheel knows the obstinacy of that type of iron steed in heading straight for any object its untrained rider wishes to avoid.

"Uncle Mark" saw that loose rock, and he saw nothing else. His wheel began to wobble while twenty feet away. He felt he was fated. The Reverend Joe coached louder and longer, seeing the unsteadiness, and finally when but a few feet away "Uncle Mark" let out a bellow: "Shut up, Joe. You ride ahead. I'm going to swear like hell in a minute."

Harold J. Barbour, New York—pp. 23–24. Helen Post Chapman remembers Twichell teaching MT to ride on a "soft clay road"; *My Hart-ford in the Nineteenth Century* (1928), 43.

499.   Mark Twain was delegated to present a certain political matter to a senator of influence at Washington. He called at the senator's office several days in succession with the vain hope of finding him at his desk; but each time was told "the senator is not in." At last he told the secretary that he had come from New York concerning an important matter, and asked if it would be possible to find the senator anywhere else, whereupon the secretary informed him that the senator was a great golfer and that likely he would find him at the X.Y. Golf Club.

Acting on the suggestion, Twain went to the Club, and inquired if the senator was there. He was told that he had "started out" about an hour ago, and should be at about the third hole. Following directions, in due time he located the senator, and after introducing himself proceeded to deliver his message, while the senator played on raising divots aplenty.

When at length Twain had delivered his message and was waiting for a reply, the senator turned toward him with flushed face and beads of honest toil standing out on his brow, and asked: "Mr. Clemens, what do you think of our golf course?" "The best I've ever tasted" was the terse reply of Mark Twain.

David Hutchinson, Connecticut—p. 24.

500.   While doing a literary composition Mark Twain required a reference book which he knew his next door neighbor had. He sent his servant over for a loan of it. His servant came back with the answer that his neighbor would be pleased to loan him it but he would have to read it in the owner's library. About a month later the neighbor sent his servant over to Mark Twain's place for a loan of his lawn mower as his had broke. He was astonished to receive the reply that Mark Twain would be pleased to lend the lawn mower, but that it must be used on the owner's lawn.

John Hood, Vancouver—p. 29. In 1926 the *Magazine of History* reported Lincoln had told this old jestbook favorite (32:extra number

125, p. 43) which, with a book instead of lawnmower, was popular in seventeenth-century London; Halliwell Phillipps, *Jokes of Cambridge Coffee-Houses in the Seventeenth Century* (1841), 30–31.

501. When submitting one of his manuscripts to the publishers, Mark Twain attached a note for them also:
"Gentlemen: .,?! ()"---*'.. Please scatter these throughout according to your taste."

Stella Randolph, Washington — p. 30.

502. As Mark Twain was crossing the Atlantic Ocean a storm came up and he was terribly seasick. Afterwards, when he was recounting the incident to a friend, he remarked: "At first you were afraid you would die and then you got so sick you were afraid you wouldn't die."

Anna Frances Nunnelley, Missouri — p. 30.

503. Among persons of distinction who used to spend their summers in Tyringham, Berkshire County, Massachusetts, were Richard Watson Gilder, Grover Cleveland and Mark Twain. Mr. Cleveland, as is well known, was a man of ample proportions. Likewise he was extremely fond of fishing. One day it was noted that Twain was not "wetting a line." A friend inquired the reason. He replied: "Cleveland is using the pond."

Joseph Hollister — p. 31.

504. At a dinner one night, finding himself the possessor of a mouthful of hot soup, he promptly turned his head and "out with it." He commented: "Some darn fools would have swallowed that."

Ibid.

1930

505. [Eighty-nine-year-old William Gillis reminisces about the fall of 1864:] Mr. Carrington, a man from Hannibal, Missouri, with his family, lived on Jackass Hill. They were in strong sympathy with the southern people then at war with the north. George Carrington had a great big Australian billy goat that he had trained to harness.

One morning . . . the old billy goat was standing looking on and Mark Twain noticed the goat and went over and said: "General, you have built up quite a reputation during this war. Now I think there is no question but that you know how to plan a battle and to carry it to a successful issue, but as a swordsman, I think you have been very greatly overrated. Now I'm going to try you out." And he went up and presented a sword and said: "On guard." And made a pass at Beauregard. Beauregard, the old general, was ready for the fray and reared up on his hind legs and hit the old sword with his horns and knocked it about twenty feet. Then he gave Mark the other horn on the side of the head and knocked him flat. Then Mark got on all fours following the old sword. It was the only time I ever heard Sam swear in earnest. He got to the old sword, brought it into the house, threw it on the floor and went out where Mr. Carrington had been watching the battle and said to him, "Carrington, what will you take for that confounded old goat?"

Said Carrington, "What do you want with him, Sam? You want to practice fencing with him?"

"Practice fencing! No, I want to kill him. He is a menace to the limbs and life of the people on the Hill. You know there are a good many children here and he is apt to kill or maim some of them very badly."

"Why, Sam?" said Carrington. "Don't you know that self-defense is the first law of nature and that you started the trouble with Beauregard? He was only working under his own right."

"The idea," said Sam, "of self-defense of a confounded goat against a man."

"Well, all the more reason," said Carrington. "He had a perfect right to defend himself and that is all he did."

Sam then came into the house and I had a bottle of Triple Horse Medicine and I made him lie down on the bed and I rubbed his neck for one-half hour, but he never bothered old Tim again. On the contrary he got friendly with General Beauregard and he and George trained another goat to work with Beauregard in harness and they used to have good times out gathering pine cones, sticks, pine-nuts, and kindling for the mother and the cabin.

William R. Gillis, *Gold Rush Days with Mark Twain* (1930), 172–74.

1931

506.   When the hours of dictation were over Father often received callers, among whom were usually a few strangers. In one instance we had a good laugh. A pathetic sort of old lady arrived, who wished to pour out her adoration for Mark Twain and his works. Before leaving, she begged permission to kiss Father's hand in reverence. Quite seriously and sympathetically he submitted to this trying compliment. At the door she said, "How God must love you!"

"I hope so," he said, but when the door had closed behind her, he added, with a wistful light in his eye, "I guess she hasn't heard of our strained relations."

Clara Clemens, *My Father Mark Twain* (1931), 259.

1933

507.   [Speaking to the caricaturist P. Richards:] "I often think that the highest compliment ever paid to my poor efforts was paid by Darwin through President Eliot of Harvard college. At least, Eliot said it was a compliment, and I always take the opinion of great men like college presidents on all such subjects as that," said Mark Twain. . . . "He went on to tell me something like this:

"'Do you know that there is one room in Darwin's house, his bedroom, where the housemaid is never allowed to touch two things? One is a plant he is growing and studying while it grows (it was one of those insect-devouring plants which consumed bugs and beetles and things for the particular delectation of Mr. Darwin), and the other some books that lie on the night table at the head of his bed. They are *your* books, Mark, and Mr. Darwin reads them every night to lull him to sleep.'

"I said: 'I regard it as a compliment and a very high honour that that great mind, labouring for the whole human race, should rest itself on *my books.* I am proud that he should read himself to sleep with them.'"

P. Richards, "Reminiscences of MT," *Library Review* 4(1933): 19–20. Speaking at the Savoy, London, in 1907, MT had alluded to a letter from Darwin to a friend: "Once I had a fine perception and appreciation of high literature, but in me that quality is atrophied." "That was the reason," said Mr. Twichell, "he was reading your books"; Fatout, 559–60.

508. [Richards recalls MT's speaking of the explorer Sir Henry Stanley:] "My books *have* had effects and very good ones, too, here and there, and some others not so good. There is no doubt about that. I remember one instance of it years and years ago: Stanley carried a book of mine feloniously away to Africa, and I have not a doubt that it had a noble and uplifting influence there in the wilds of the dark continent — because in his previous journeys he never carried anything to read except Shakespeare and the Bible. I didn't know that he had carried a book of mine. I only noticed that when he came back he was a reformed man."

Richards, 20–21.

509. [Responding to a reporter's queries, Jehovah says that MT has "a river of his own in Heaven — or, in fact, anywhere he wants it":] "You never saw such a spectacle as one of Mark's steamboat races, with Mark on the deck of the winning ship, archangels, saints and devils lined up on the banks of the river shouting and cheering, the boats belching fire and smoke, and Mark making the welkin ring with profanity. . . .

"Mark ran his river, with one of his most exciting races going on, right through the middle of Hell one time, and Satan turned blue with envy and admiration. He said that for pure *style* and interest it laid over anything he could invent. He came and begged me to let him have Mark and his river for a while. I put it up to Mark, and he was all for going. But he didn't go, in the end."

"Why not?"

"His wife and William Dean Howells wouldn't let him," said Jehovah. "They said it would look bad . . . people wouldn't understand . . . either you were respectable, or you weren't. And Mark said if people didn't quit editing him, he'd go to Hell and stay there. But he won't. He wouldn't get any fun out of it, if he were there all the time. He needs contrast. Everybody does. I need it myself. That's the reason I let him take his river anywhere he wants to."

Don Marquis, *Chapters for the Orthodox* (1933), 138–39.

1934

510. Once Mark was with his most intimate friend, the Reverend Doctor Joseph H. Twichell, and he began to swear with his usual fluency, when Twichell asked him to stop, saying it really wasn't necessary for him to be quite so profane. "Oh, Joe," said Mark, "you and I use exactly the same words, you in your prayers and I in my conversation; but we don't either of us mean anything by it."

William Lyon Phelps, "As I Like It," *Scribner's Magazine* 95 (June 1934): 434.

1935

The next half-dozen entries are from Cyril Clemens, *MT Wit and Wisdom* (1935), an expansion of his earlier *MT Anecdotes,* entries 478–504, issued perhaps for the Twain centennial.

511. When in England Mark Twain used to tell the story of a fellow-countryman of his whose name was James Tod. He was invited to dinner by a lady who spelled his name with two "d's." The evening of the dinner, the gentleman told the hostess that she had made a mistake by spelling his name with two "d's." She said that she thought he ought really to spell his name with two "d's." She had several friends by the name of Todd, and they all used the double "d"; "spelled with only one, it looks like, what shall I say — a mouth with one tooth missing? A man with a short limb? Anyhow, it looks incomplete!"

"Perhaps so, ma'am," he replied, "but God Almighty has managed to jog along, thus far, with only one 'd' to his name, and what is good enough for God Almighty is good enough for plain Jim Tod!"

P. 72. In MT's lifetime this circulated as an Abe Lincoln story; *AL Laughing*, 136.

512.   Irving Cobb tells this story:
A young reporter called one morning as the great humorist lay reading and smoking in bed, and announced that he would like his life-story for his newspaper. Mark Twain took a draw on his pipe and commenced:
"Well, in the days of King George the Third when I was a young man I used—"
"Pardon me, right there," interrupted the reporter. "I know that you are not a spring chicken, but how could you possibly have been living during the time of George the Third?"
"Fine, young man," returned Mark, smilingly offering the young man a cigar, "I heartily congratulate you. You are the first and only reporter I have ever met in my whole life who corrected a mistake *before* it appeared in print."

P. 83.

513.   Eli Perkins describes being at a party with Mark Twain, Joaquin Miller and others. Each had told a sea story, and Mark was asked to tell one too.
"A true story?" asked the humorist.
"Why, of course," replied everyone.
"Well, gentlemen," Mark Twain began with his wonderful drawl, and told them how he crossed the Atlantic on one of the stoutest ships of the Anchor Line. Suddenly one morning a terrific storm came up, and billows monstrous high dashed over the vessel, the masts were blown overboard and then the rudder went. All of a sudden the ship settled and went down with every soul on board.
After the wonder had somewhat subsided, Joaquin Miller, the poet, came up to the humorist and said:
"You did not tell us how you escaped, Mr. Twain."

"I didn't escape!" exclaimed Twain. "I went down with the rest."

P. 88.

514. Norman Hapgood tells how, in conversation, Mark Twain commented on the tendency of people in New York and the East in general to talk all the time about money matters, and contrasted it with his own home in the West, saying:

"Now, in Hannibal, Missouri, where I was brought up, we never talked about money. There was not enough money in the place to furnish a topic of conversation."

Pp. 94–95. A more succinct version in C. Clemens' *MT's Jest Book* (1963), 20, omits the reference to money.

515. One day during his last visit to London, in 1907, Mark Twain was visiting Madame Tussaud's Wax Works. Intent upon studying some strange and grotesque figure in the Chamber of Horrors, he was suddenly recalled to reality by a violent stab in the ribs. Turning angrily around, he was just in time to see a stout ruddy-cheeked English matron withdrawing her umbrella and then making off with the remark:

"I *thought* he wasn't wax!"

P. 162.

516. A friend once wrote Mark Twain a letter saying that he was in very wretched health, and concluding, "Is there anything worse than having toothache and earache at the same time?"

The humorist wrote back promptly that even worse was to have rheumatism and Saint Vitus' dance simultaneously.

P. 167.

1937

517. When I was a boy of 14, my father was so ignorant I could hardly stand to have the old man around. But when I got to be

21, I was astonished at how much he had learned in 7 years.—
Mark Twain.

"Bringing Up Father," *Reader's Digest* 31 (Sept. 1937): 22. This old
favorite could not be authentic "fact," since his father died before MT
was twelve.

1939

518. [Recalling a dinner at Richard Watson Gilder's home:] Mr.
Gilder told us he feared we should see little of Mark, as Mrs.
Clemens had recently died and the blow to the great humorist
had been tragic. That night at dinner, however, as our gay party
were laughing and jesting, Mark, with his shock of white hair,
walked in. We were surprised and delighted. Nevertheless, our
gaiety ceased as he sat down between me and Mrs. Gilder.

"What are you talking about?" he asked in the pause. I answered, "Names—funny names of people." He waited a moment,
then said with a drawling grin, "Well, I knew a girl out in Missouri who had twenty-four Christian names—and they called her
'Puss.'"

Cale Young Rice, *Bridging the Years* (1939), pp. 94–95.

1940

The next twenty-two entries are from Opie Read's posthumous *Mark
Twain and I* (1940), a collection by his sons of anecdotes in the Chicago
Daily News the previous winter. Read died, "nearly eighty-seven," in
1939. He had known Mark Twain when Read himself had been a young
reporter.

519. A militant reformer had cornered Mark Twain in a Kansas
hotel, and, as I approached, it was apparent that the great humorist was being held down to an occasional exclamation.

"We finally cleared demon rum out of the state," the reformer
was saying. "Day after day—week after week—month after month

of indefatigable labor finally produced its sterling reward. We never let up for one moment. We finally got rid of liquor.

"Yes, sir, we went after liquor and we got rid of it.

"And when we've banished liquor from every state in the Union, we're going after tobacco."

Mark Twain reached into his pocket, took out his pipe, stood up, glanced toward the tobacco counter and said: "Good. I'm going after some now."

P. 7.

520.   In a Denver hotel I found almost thrilling amusement while listening to a conversation between Mark Twain and Anderson Gibbs, a man internationally known for his promotion of music.

"Music," said Gibbs, "is about the oldest of all the arts."

"Yes, older than the human race," Mark Twain agreed. "The cave man shouted his music before he could jabber his mystifying conception of life."

"Music is strength," continued Gibbs.

"As to that, I'm not so sure," interrupted Mark Twain. "The strongest man I ever saw was a deck hand on a Mississippi River steamboat. He could carry a bale of cotton but he couldn't carry a tune."

P. 12.

521.   "Oh, Mr. Mark Twain," exclaimed Miss Gertrude Andrews, a beginner in writing whom I had introduced to the humorist after one of his lectures, "I'm just reading your 'Life on the Mississippi.' Some of the episodes are so gruesome!"

"Episodes that are gruesome to some people may be actually funny to others," replied the humorist. "Take the case of Ed Johnson, a sheriff down in Arkansas. During logging time quite a number of bodies came floating down the river. As Ed usually took immediate charge on such occasions, he was known in the community as 'First Search Johnson.' On Saturday nights he was usually to be found in the town's best saloon spending damp money.

"One day the boys brought ashore a particularly well-dressed victim. Johnson reached in one of the victim's pockets and took out a $20 note. In another pocket he found a pistol. 'That's bad,' he remarked. 'I'll just fine this man this $20 for carrying this pistol.'"

P. 22. Myron W. Tracy attributes this to Judge Roy Bean; "Roy Bean: Law West of the Pecos," *Straight Texas: Publications of the Texas Folk-Lore Society* 13 (1937): 113. Tracy adds that Bean denied the story, saying it confused another incident in which he did appropriate ten dollars from a dead shooting victim to keep it from going to waste.

522. "You are one of the most unconscious of philosophers," Mark Twain once said to [Ellis Grimp]. Old Grimp smiled. "I don't know exactly what you mean, but I reckon it's all right."

"Easy enough to explain," said Mark Twain. "It is said that years ago, down at Natchez, you got into an argument with a man of active intelligence, known far and wide as Davy Crockett, and that after a spirited mental contest, you and Crockett seized each other in a furious wrestling bout. Lawyers, and even the judge, ran out of the courthouse to look upon the contest, and when you had thrown Crockett the judge invited you into the courthouse and presented you with a mint julep."

Old Glimp looked about him and softly laughed. "Mister," he said, "I've told that story until sometimes I almost believe it myself. Did you ever try to make yourself believe a lie?"

"Yes, when I sought to convince myself that certain politicians were honest."

"Did you ever meet a man that was absolutely honest?"

"Yes, undoubtedly."

"And did you talk to him, Mr. Twain?"

"Well, hardly. He hadn't been honest but a short time. I was attending his funeral."

P. 22.

523. At an old canopied well in the hills of Kentucky, Mark Twain and I stopped to refresh ourselves, drinking directly from a large, oaken bucket swung on a chain and pulley.

"Education seems not to have disturbed the thoughts of these contented people until recently," observed Mark Twain. "That school house down yonder is new."

"Yes, sir, it is new," said a picturesque old negro who had just stepped up to get a drink, "and we're mighty proud of it. My little grandson goes to it. The other day he wrote a letter to his aunt up in Cincinnati. He has an uncle way up in New York, but he can't write that far yet."

P. 25.

524. [MT recalls an ingenious trick by Major Banister, a Missouri innkeeper:] At the Major's inn there came for a night's lodging, Rutherford Foster and Sam Stiles, rivals for state senator in that district. The Major made them believe that the inn was so crowded that they would have to share the same room, even the same bed.

When they were about to retire, the Major called Foster to one side and said, "Hope you don't have any trouble, but the truth is that Stiles has nightmares. The only way to quiet him is to bark like a dog. Then he goes right to sleep."

A little later the Major called Stiles to one side and said, "Foster is all right except that he has nightmares and barks like a dog. His family doctor has informed me that the only way to quiet him is to stroke him with a comb."

Along about midnight, Foster began to bark like a dog, whereupon Stiles raked him with a comb, and the turmoil began.

The next day the Major went from place to place recounting this ridiculous episode with such telling effect that the Major himself was elected to the office.

P. 26. The basic joke can be traced as far back as the sixteenth-century French jestbook, *Mirror of Mirth*; P.M. Zall, *Hundred Merry Tales* (1963), 382–84.

525. "How far should a community go in giving assistance to the needy?" asked one of our party as we were riding in the smoking compartment with Mark Twain, on the way to New York. "It seems to me," continued the speaker, "that if you do too much for them you make them lazy."

"I remember a dog I had," replied Mark Twain. "Just to humor him one time when he was scratching, I did the scratching for him, in the right places, and he was surprised and pleased.

"After that he seemed to expect me to help him out in the same way, which I did. And would you believe it, he finally got so he wouldn't do any of his own scratching at all! He would come up to me and merely point with his nose or his paw to the place he wanted scratched.

"Now the point is that it wasn't laziness, for he would chase rabbits all day. It was simply a matter of habit."

P. 31.

526. In a reminiscent trip up the old river, Mark Twain was looking toward a stop-over at an old landing which once had flashed forth the bright light of romance. Shortly after arriving, as we rested in a tavern sitting room, there came a tapping on the side of the open door. In came a tall young man.

"Mr. Clemens," said the visitor, "I am a newspaper reporter and have been commissioned to ask a few questions. What is humor?"

"The good natured side of any truth," Mark Twain answered.

"What are the past and the future?"

"For the majority of us, the past is a regret; the future an experiment."

"And what is man's most universal weakness?"

"Lying," the humorist answered.

The visitor rose. "Sir, you move me to tell the truth. I am not a reporter. I resorted to a deception just to meet you."

Mark Twain smiled, "A man is never more truthful than when he acknowledges himself a liar. I am glad to meet you, sir. Wait a moment. When I say that, I am a liar, too. And now, let two liars shake hands."

P. 34.

527. My friend Lou Carruthers had several times expressed his desire to meet Mark Twain, and I finally found occasion to introduce him to the genius of mirth at a New York restaurant.

Carruthers was quite a fisherman and I could see that he was looking for an opening to get in one of his incredible stories. "Well, that reminds me of the time we started out tarpon fishing," launched forth Carruthers, while nothing had been said that could possibly remind him.

"By the way," broke in Mark Twain, "I've got to go out West again. The last time I was out in Colorado we were driving along a dangerously narrow mountain road in a stage coach, with a sheer wall on one side and a sheer drop of a thousand feet on the other, when suddenly the horses stopped and r'ared up. Right there on the road ahead of us was one of the biggest rattlesnakes I've ever seen. It had already struck, luckily hitting the tongue of the coach. The stage driver, a crack shot, fired betwen the horses' heads and killed the snake.

"As we continued on our way I noticed that the horses were walking further and further apart. And then I saw that the coach tongue, where the rattlesnake had bitten it, had swollen up as big around as a barrel. And then—"

Carruthers broke in. "Pardon me, Mr. Twain, er—pardon me—I just don't think that is true."

"Well," returned Mark Twain rising, "I've heard of your fish stories and I just wanted to head one of them off with a snake story."

P. 35.

528. "I suppose you've seen many a duel, Mr. Clemens," said old Nate Tinsley, proprietor of a Kentucky roadside inn.

"Yes, and some pretty strange ones," replied the humorist. "One night two young blades got into an argument over a village charmer who had just received a new dress from a large mail order concern. They decided to go to a log cabin and fight it out with pistols, in the dark. Thus, they entered the dark one-room cabin, drew their pistols and started crowding behind chairs and tables.

"Finally, one of the duelists began to get soft-hearted. 'Aw, I don't want to kill him,' he said to himself. 'He's a good fellow. Guess I'll fire my pistol once and call the whole thing off.' Then he proceeded to maneuver to a suitable place to shoot his pistol.

He came to the fireplace, and, thrusting his pistol up the chimney, he fired . . . and down came his rival."

P. 40.

529. "Mr. Clemens," asked one of my fellow reporters as we of the press were interviewing the great humorist, "do you think that raising the price of gold would lead to inflation?" This question was just as much a matter of interest many years ago as it is today.

"Who knows what leads to what?" returned Mark Twain. "Reminds me of a time when I was strolling through the backwoods of Missouri. I came to a clearing where there was a cabin and a fence, and I was startled by scores of hogs running wildly about the clearing.

"An old man stood leaning against the fence. I asked him what all the commotion was about.

"'I lost my voice a while ago,' said the old man in a thin, squeaky tone. When I asked him what difference that made, he said, 'Well, I got to calling my hogs for feeding by tapping on the fence with my pipe. Everything was all right until a few days ago, when the blamed woodpeckers got on to it and now they're running my hogs to death.'"

P. 43.

530. "Which do you think is right, Mr. Twain?" asked a rather attractive school mistress of the celebrated humorist, after he had delivered a lecture in Chicago and was preparing to accept of our hospitality. "Do you believe in a high or a low tariff?"

"Now you're getting into something," replied Mark Twain.

"Well, I notice," continued the school mistress, "that when there's a high tariff I'm out of a job, and when there's a low tariff I have a job."

"That reminds me," returned Mark Twain, "of an old man I met out in Iowa who had come up from Arkansas. I asked him whether he had experienced much cold during the preceding winter, and he exclaimed, 'Cold! If the thermometer had been an inch longer we'd all have frozen to death!'"

P. 44.

531. With Warren Harding, who doubtless had no thought at that time of ever being president, Mark Twain and I sat at a table in a prairie restaurant.

"There is nothing more painstaking than pretending honesty," remarked Mark Twain.

"I suppose," said Harding, "that you have in mind men who make it a point to advertise their honesty?"

"Yes," replied Mark Twain, "I remember an old man who kept a toll gate in Missouri. One day he and his son were working in a field, having left the toll gate open. Along came a man on a horse. He could have ridden on, but seeing the old fellow out in the field, he got down, tied his horse and trudged on out to where the old man was hoeing. 'Your toll gate is open,' he said, 'but I didn't want to beat my way through. Here's your 10 cents toll fare.'

"'I forgot to close it,' said the old man. 'And did you come all the way over this dusty field to give me 10 cents?'

"'Yes, sir,' returned the traveler.

"The old man turned toward his son and called out, 'Here, Steve; watch this fellow. He'll steal somethin' before he gits off the place.'"

P. 45. So far as I can find, not even Cyril Clemens, who also collected Harding letters, thought of pairing MT and the future president as his straight man.

532. The old Mississippi had risen so high that it was a matter of news. Seeking a story for my newspaper, I had the good fortune at Natchez to run into Mark Twain.

Of course, the conversation centered around the high waters and each person present tried to outdo the others in recalling how high he had seen the Mississippi at one time or another.

Jim Britside said he had seen it fifty miles wide at Natchez. Boyd Shirley said that some tall pines in his yard on a hill still bore the marks of driftwood on their topmost boughs.

Mark Twain listened until each had put in his proud and bragging recollection. Then he spoke: "Gentlemen, you don't know what a wide river is. I've seen this river so wide that it had only one bank."

P. 48.

533.   On entering the smoking compartment of a southbound train I was delighted to find Mark Twain with his usual group of fascinated listeners. He was on a lecture tour and the conversation soon led to audiences.

"An audience likes a speaker with the same weaknesses and the same virtues as they themselves have," said Mark Twain. "If the lecturer's brow is too high and the brows of the audience are too low, look out. Or, if a high-brow audience sees a low-brow lecturer there's trouble.

"Old Colonel Vischer had the right idea. He wore a wig. Just before time to go on the platform, he would peep through at the wings to get an estimate of the intellectuality of his audience. If it were a low-brow audience, he would pull his wig down over his forehead. If a high-brow audience, he would push his wig back. Worked fine. Always made a favorable impression on his audience, until one night he lost his wig."

"What happened?" asked a trainman.

"Went over bigger than ever," returned Mark. "There was a big institution in town to treat baldness, and the audience were mostly bald-headed men who had come to town to take the treatment."

P. 53. The authenticity of this story is suspect because the *Oxford English Dictionary* dates the introduction of the term *highbrow* in this sense from 1906.

534.   [At an Indianapolis hotel, James Whitcomb Riley asks:] "And now, Mark Twain, what is your conception of humor?"

"The question has been asked of me a thousand times, Brother Riley, but each time I try to give a different answer. This time, let me say that humor is a sudden light on the funny side of things that often keeps one from saying or doing something foolish."

"True enough," said Riley. "It seems to me that even a dog at times can see the funny side of things."

"Certainly," Mark Twain returned. "Tell a dog a joke and he never fails to wag his tail. I had a dog that would wag himself from one side of the road to the other whenever I introduced him to a politician."

P. 57.

535. An old Mississippi River boat flashed her elegance as we sat on the upper deck, encircling Mark Twain. . . . A heavy step caused us to turn, and up came a huge man. Soot and grime marked his features, while his clothes looked as though they had been worn by a mule that worked in a coal mine.

"Told the old lady I'd shake your hand and now I've got to," said the roustabout. "Pardon me if my mit is greasy but I've just been cleaning a mess of catfish."

"Pardon me, too," said Mark Twain, grasping the boatman's hand. "Just getting over a touch of leprosy, myself."

P. 59.

536. Practically every member of the Chicago Press Club had gathered in the lobby to greet Mark Twain, scheduled to attend a luncheon given in his honor.

As the champion of hilarity entered, surrounded by a committee, the members cried, "Speech! Speech!"

Not wishing to draw upon the humorous words which he had prepared for the luncheon, Mark Twain raised his hand for silence.

"Gentlemen," he said, "this reminds me of old Jed Thomas, back in Missouri, said to have been one of the Younger Brothers' gang. He was standing under a tree waiting for the sheriff's boys to get the rope properly adjusted over a limb when the sheriff asked him if he had anything to say.

"'I've stolen lots of hosses, I admit,' said Jed, 'I've robbed trains and I might add that I've killed a dozen sheriffs or so. But I ain't got nothing to say on this here occasion. I just don't feel in the mood to make a speech. Words don't come just right. I couldn't do myself justice, and I don't want to hurt my reputation.'"

P. 61.

537. Mark Twain and I were in Springfield, to muse along the pathway so often strode by Lincoln and were sitting in the shade of a spreading tree where the Great Emancipator had, no doubt, often sat, when up came Billy Mason, a man active in Congress. Billy Mason spoke:

"Mr. Clemens, I have often thought what a pity it was that fate did not intend that Lincoln should marry Ann Rutledge. It seems that fate governs our lives and plans history in advance."

"Yes," Mark Twain responded, "had Lincoln married the dear one of his heart's love he might have led a happy but obscure life and the world would never have heard of him. Happiness seeks obscurity to enjoy itself. A good-looking milkmaid might have kept Alexander the Great from conquering the world."

"Well, doesn't that prove," asked Billy Mason, "that what is to be will be?"

"The only thing it proves to me," returned Mark Twain, "is that what has been was."

P. 62. Conceivably the straight man is the William Ernest Mason who represented Chicago in Congress (1887–91) and Illinois in the Senate (1897–1903).

538. We were steaming up the river on the old and sighing "Natchez." Mark Twain had sat for a long time in reminiscent silence when up came an old fellow by the name of John Woodsen of Vicksburg.

"Mr. Clemens, what in your opinion was the most humorously apt answer to a question ever made?"

Mark Twain replied: "A man wrote to the editor of London *Punch* and asked, 'Is life worth living?'

"Then came the answer, now known all over the world—'It depends upon the liver.'

"But that does not embrace the whole of the human family. Had the question been asked of a cynic, he would not have said that life depends upon the liver but the gall bladder."

P. 63.

539. Well do I remember a talk between Mark Twain and blind Senator [Thomas] Gore of Oklahoma.

"It seems," remarked the senator, "that no one knows exactly what is good fortune or bad fortune, until long after it happens. I've often thought that if I were not blind I should not be in the United States Senate today."

"That reminds me," said Mark Twain, "of Jim Watrous, who lived down in Missouri many years ago. His one big ambition was to be representative in the state legislature. But he used such big words when he made a speech that nobody in his farming district could understand him. His election seemed very doubtful.

"One evening he was milking a cow and practising one of his speeches at the same time, when the cow kicked him in the jaw, causing him to bite off the end of his tongue."

"Well that," returned Senator Gore, "must have put an end to his career as a politician."

"Not at all," answered Mark Twain. "After that he could use only words of one syllable and that made such a hit with the farmers that he was elected."

P. 64. Blind since boyhood, Sen. Gore served in the U.S. Senate 1907–21 and again 1931–37.

540. [Recording an illustration MT used for the saying, "Misery loves company":] Two old fellows were crossing a log that spanned a creek. Suddenly one of them slipped and fell in. The water came up to his neck and his feet were held securely by mud. His friend leaned down to try to pull him up but he could not quite reach him. Then he got a stick and tugged and tugged but the fellow in the water could not extricate his feet. After several hours of hard work, the man who was high and dry said, "Luke, I guess I can't get you out. But, I'll tell you what I'll do; I'll get down in there with you."

P. 70.

541. [Alluding to a newspaper interview with Margot Asquith, who told about meeting MT in 1907 when he:] "told me of a great American temperance orator who before speaking at a meeting, had asked the chairman to provide milk, instead of water, for his use while speaking. The chairman put rum into the milk, said Mark Twain, and the orator, at a dramatic period in his speech, first took a sip of the milk and then, eying it appreciatively, tossed off the entire contents of the glass. Putting it down slowly he exhaled a deep breath and exclaimed: 'Gosh! What cows!'"

Twainian 2 (Apr. 1940): 6. Mody C. Boatright, *Folk Laughter on the American Frontier* (1949), 144, gives it as a story about an itinerant Methodist preacher who exclaims, "O Lord, what a cow!" That story is not connected with MT.

542.   One bright spring afternoon I met him at the crowded corner of Fifth Avenue and 42nd St. As usual we stopped to exchange our customary banter about the ignorance of youth and the impotence of age. Thousands and thousands of men, women and children passed us and every mother's son and daughter turned his or her head to look at the picturesque figure. Some of them stopped and listened. At one time there must have been fifteen or twenty typical New York rufuses gawking at him. Mark loved it. His face was aflame. His eyes shone. He talked better and louder than I had ever heard him. Finally I said, "Let's get out of here and go over to the Century and have a drink."

"I'm not a member of the Century. What's the matter with staying here?"

"But aren't you embarrassed standing here in these crowds, talking to a celebrity?" I said.

He answered like a man coming out of a trance. His eyes were wide open and staring. He stammered: "Wh-wh-why, do *you* think these people are looking at *you*? Why, you conceited fellow, they're looking at *me*!" Then the fact dawned on him that youth had at last rebelled. His face broke into a great grin. "Oh, come on over to the Century and have a drink."

"But you just said you weren't a member."

"I'm not. That makes my hospitality all the more remarkable. What could be finer than to entertain a friend at a club where you're not a member?"

"But I'm a member."

"I knew that or I wouldn't have invited you."

Memoir by P.F. Dunne in Elmer Ellis, *Mr. Dooley's America* (1941),

195–96. The complete memoir, ed. Philip Dunne (1963), adds a concluding phrase, "to have a drink" and subsequent foolery about charg-
ing the drinks to Henry Rogers (251).

1942

543.   My contact with him really began many years ago, when
I was quite a young man. I had finished an absorbed reading of
his short stories—"The Jumping Frog" and many others. Among
them was one on "The Siamese Twins"—those two unhappy mor-
tals who were unseverably joined by a cruel ligament into per-
petual companionship. He described their troubles, one of which
was that one of them, having fallen in love, insisted on moonlight walks with his inamorata, although the other was crippled
with inflammatory rheumatism. Then, at the end of the tale, he
remarked: "Having forgotten to mention it sooner, I will remark
in conclusion that the ages of the Siamese Twins are respectively
fifty-one and fifty-three years."
   I wrote him that I had read this story with deep emotion, but
that I was utterly nonplussed by this concluding statement and
would like him to clear it up. Promptly he replied:

> My dear Church:
>   That was a blunder of mine, an egregious blunder, and
> one peculiarly calculated to confuse and mislead. What I
> meant to say was that the twins were born at the same time
> but of different mothers.

Samuel Harden Church letter to Cyril Clemens, 19 Feb. 1942, rpt.
MTJ 17 (1974–75): outside back cover.

1944

544.   He invented the story of a bank president who was proud
of a glass eye that had been made for him by the greatest artist
in Paris. "Twain, you need $5,000," he quoted this gentleman.
"I'll give it to you if you can guess which of my eyes is the glass

one." "It's the left one, of course," snapped Twain. "It's the only one with a glint of human kindness in it."

Bennet Cerf, *Try and Stop Me* (1944), rpt. *Bumper Crop* (1952), 1: 600.

545. Another friend was the sort who would punctuate a story at least three times with, "Now stop me if you've heard this one before." Twain grew impatient one day and assured him, "I not only heard your damn story, I made it up!"

Ibid., 602.

1948

546. A hypocritical business pirate once told Twain, "Before I die I mean to make a pilgrimage to the Holy Land. I will climb to the top of Mount Sinai and read the Ten Commandments aloud." "I have a better idea," said Twain. "Why don't you stay right at home in Boston and keep them?"

Bennet Cerf, *Shake Well Before Using* (1948); rpt. *Bumper Crop*, 2: 525.

547. In Richmond one day, Twain complained of an acute pain in his head. "It can't be the air or the food you ate in Richmond," said a native son confidently. "There's no healthier city than Richmond. Our death rate is down to one person a day." "Run down to the newspaper office," begged Twain, "and find out if today's victim has died yet."

Ibid.

1963

The next dozen entries are from Cyril Clemens, *Mark Twain's Jest Book* (1963), an expansion of his *MT Anecdotes* (1929) and *MT Wit and Wisdom* (1935).

548. Out walking in Hartford one day Mark was approached by a tramp. "Could you give a fellow the price of something to eat, sir?"

"You unfortunate man," sympathized Mark. "Come on, I'll buy you a drink."

"I don't drink sir."

"How about a cigar?"

"Look, sir, I'm hungry and besides I never in my life smoked."

"How would you like me to place a couple of dollars for you tomorrow on a sure-winner horse?"

"Maybe I've done lots of things wrong, but I never gamble," replied the derelict somewhat proudly. "Say, sir, hadn't you better cut all this talk and give me a nickle for a cup of coffee?"

"Tell you what," answered Mark with sudden inspiration. "I'll stake you to a whole dinner if you let me introduce you to Mrs. Clemens. I want to show her what becomes of a fellow who doesn't smoke, drink or gamble!"

P. 1.

549.   Meeting Mark after he had acquired an interest in a publishing house, a friend asked him how things were going.

"Splendidly," replied Mark enthusiastically. "I was rarely fortunate to be let in on the ground floor!"

After the collapse of the venture, the same friend consoled him and expressed surprise. "How did it possibly happen? You told me you were let in on the ground floor!"

"So I was," returned Mark ruefully, "but there was a son-of-a——— *in the basement!*"

P. 4.

550.   At some dinner party Mark was seated next to an erudite bespectacled blue stocking who confided when the sugar was passed, "Did you ever stop to think, Mr. Twain, that *sugar* and *sumac* are the only words in our language with *su* having the *sh* sound?"

To which Mark drily replied, "Are you quite *sure?*"

Ibid. Cyril Clemens adds: "When Bennet Cerf erroneously attributed the above anecdote to Bernard Shaw the Editor wrote to the latter who promptly replied in a hand marvelously legible for a man of eighty-nine: 'It must have been Mark, as 'sure' is the American form of assent, not the English one (nor the Irish).'" Still, the pun has been attributed to Rudyard Kipling in R. Thurston Hopkins, *Rudyard Kipling* (3d ed. 1921), 82.

551.   While visiting New Zealand on a lecture tour in the late nineties, Mark Twain found that the trains were exceedingly slow-moving. One day he was caught on a train that seemed unusually deliberate and creeping—even for New Zealand. When the conductor finally came around, Mark promptly handed him half a ticket which was customarily used for juvenile passengers. The official looked hard at the white-haired, bushy moustached humorist in no little surprise, and demanded somewhat sarcastically, "And are you a child?"

"No, not any more," replied Mark blandly, "but I was when I got on your damn train!"

P. 5. In "The Editor's Drawer," *Harper's Monthly* 35 (June 1867): 134, the version is about "last winter's snowstorm" between Syracuse and Oswego when the conductor maintains, "This boy is too large to travel for half-fare." The parent replies: "He wasn't when he started!"

552.   One summer Mark was spending a holiday in Maine, and he remarked to an old fisherman, "I do not feel very well this morning. I wish you would get an Osteopath for me and bring him up."

The old man replied that he had been a fisherman there for thirty years but had never caught one yet!

The next day Mark was much amused to learn that, that night the old man told his wife about it, and she informed him that he was all wrong—an Osteopath was not a fish, but a bird.

P. 7.

553.   While at his summer residence just outside of Elmira Mark prepared one evening to take a drive, and expecting to remain out until late, told the stable boy that he need not wait up for him. He directed the fellow, however, when he had finished his work to lock the stable and place the key under the stone, the location of which Clemens described with much exactness. When the humorist reached home after his drive, he was surprised to find the key was not in the place selected. When his patience had become exhausted, he awoke the boy who explained, as he started out to locate the missing key: "Mr. Clemens, I found *a better place to hide it.*"

P. 8.

554. One day when Sam was a lad working on a Hannibal paper, an old man came in and wanted his permanent cure for drunkenness, the apple cure, published in the paper. After the fellow had expatiated for a while on the wonderful effectiveness of his cure, Sam asked, "You believe in it, then, do you, Hank?"

"Believe in it?" was the prompt reply. "How can I help believing in it? Ain't it cured me twenty-seven times already?"

P. 9.

555. Miss Dora Wheeler writes the editor that Mark once called at their home, but failed to notice the new-fangled push button that had just been installed. After failing to rouse anyone by knuckle-knocking, he scribbled a note which he slipped under the door: "Where in Hell is the bell?"

P. 11.

556. One year when Mark Twain attended a New Year's party, the subject of resolutions very naturally became a topic of conversation.

"Are you making any resolutions this year, Mark?" someone asked.

"You bet," replied the writer. "I'm going to live within my income this year even if I have to borrow money to do it."

P. 18.

557. Mark always got a big kick out of literature discussions.

"Have you read any of Miss So-and-so's novels?" someone asked him.

"Yes, a few," admitted the humorist.

"What do you think of her latest book?" persisted the other.
"Once you put it down," commented Twain, "you simply can't pick it up."

P. 18.

558. One year Mark Twain did some post season fishing in Maine and upon his way back to Boston that night he could not resist bragging about the twelve beautiful fish he had caught, to an affable gentleman who was sitting next to him.

Finally the gentleman said to Mark, "You know who I am?"
Twain answered, "No, I don't" and the gentleman said, "I am the Maine Game Warden."

Mark in turn said, "You don't seem to know who I am," and the Warden's answer was, "No."

Said Mark: "I am the damnedest liar on earth."

P. 21. This exchange was supposed to have taken place between H.L. Woods and a Colorado game warden in *After Dinner Stories and Repartee* (1908), 38.

559. "You Missouri people are all right," a New Yorker once said to Mark Twain, "but you're too provincial."

"Provincial?" snorted Mark. "On the contrary. Nobody in New York knows anything about Missouri, but everybody in Missouri knows all about New York."

P. 26. The same story with no connection to MT and with the setting in Chicago appears in Vance Randolph, *Hot Springs and Hell* (1965), 194–95.

Sources

[Numbers in brackets refer to entries.]
An exhaustive list of secondary sources may be found in Thomas A. Tenney, *Mark Twain: A Reference Guide* (Boston: G.K. Hall, 1977).

Alta California (San Francisco). 13 May, 20 May, 4 August 1867. [18–20, 22]
Atlantic Monthly. Boston: H.O. Houghton. Vols. 37–40 (1876–77). [50, 58]
Ayers, James. J. *Gold and Sunshine.* Boston: Badger, 1922. [456]
Bacheller, Irving. *Coming Up the Road.* Indianapolis: Bobbs-Merrill, 1928. [472]
Bainton, George. *The Art of Authorship.* London: J. Clarke, 1890. [99]
Bookman. New York: Bookman Publishing, Vol. 31 (1910). [419]
Budd, Louis J. "Interviews with Mark Twain." *ALR* 10 (1977): 1–100. [159]

Californian, The. San Francisco: A. Roman. Vol. 4 (1881). [70]
Cerf, Bennet. *Bumper Crop of Anecdotes and Stories.* 2 vols. Garden City, N.Y.: Garden City Books, 1952. [544–47]
Clemens, Clara. *My Father Mark Twain.* New York: Harper, 1931. [506]
Clemens, Cyril, ed. *Mark Twain Anecdotes.* Webster Groves, Mo.: Mark Twain Society, 1929. [478–504]
_____. *Mark Twain's Jest Book.* Kirkwood, Mo., 1963. [548–59]
_____. *Mark Twain Wit and Wisdom.* New York: Stokes, 1935. [511–16]
Clemens, Samuel L. *Autobiography,* ed. Albert Bigelow Paine. 2 vols. New York: Harper, 1924. [280, 369, 385]
_____. *Celebrated Jumping Frog of Calaveras County, and Other Sketches.* New York: C.H. Webb, 1867. [21]
_____. "Chapters from My Autobiography." *North American Review* 184 (March 1907): 561–71. [393]
_____. *Date 1601.* West Point, N.Y.: Ye Academie Presse, 1882. [51–57]
_____. *Early Tales and Sketches,* ed. Edgar M. Branch and Robert Hirst. Berkeley: University of California Press, 1979. [1, 4, 5, 7]
_____. *Following the Equator.* Hartford, Conn.: American Publishing, 1897. [165–240]
_____. *The Innocents Abroad, or the New Pilgrims' Progress.* Hartford, Conn.: American Publishing, 1869. [28–29]

_____. "Last Lotus Club Speech." *After Dinner Speeches at the Lotus Club.* New York: Lotus Club, 1911. [401]

_____. *Letters,* ed. Albert Bigelow Paine. 2 vols. New York: Harper, 1917. [82]

_____. *Life on the Mississippi.* Boston: Osgood, 1883. [75]

_____. *Mark Twain-Howells Letters,* ed. Henry Nash Smith and William M. Gibson. Cambridge, Mass.: Harvard University Press, 1960. [64]

_____. Mark Twain Papers typescripts. Bancroft Library, University of California, Berkeley. [113, 147]

_____. *Mark Twain Speaking* [speeches], ed. Paul Fatout. Iowa City: Univ. of Iowa Press, 1976. [86, 104, 160, 279, 286, 291–94, 388, 391, 397]

_____. *Mark Twain's Notebook,* ed. Albert Bigelow Paine. New York: Harper, 1935. [101, 118–19, 161–63, 241–77, 300–321, 370–80, 389–90, 403]

_____. *Mark Twain's Speeches,* intro. William Dean Howells. New York: Harper, 1910. [287, 290, 383–84, 386–87, 405–407]

_____. *Mark Twain's Speeches,* intro. William Dean Howells. New York: Harper, 1923. [278]

_____. "To My Missionary Critics." *North American Review* 172 (April 1901): 520–34. [288]

_____. *Notebooks and Journals,* ed. Frederick Anderson, et al. Berkeley: University of California Press, 1975–. 4 vols. [8–17, 23–27, 49, 59–63, 65–67, 71–74, 76–78, 81, 83–85, 87–91, 93–96, 100–103]

_____. *£1,000,000 Bank-Note and Other New Stories.* New York: Charles L. Webster, 1893. [97–98]

_____. "Pudd'nhead Wilson." *Century.* Vols. 47–48 (1893–94). [132–46]

_____. *Pudd'nhead Wilson's Calendar for 1894.* [New York: Century, 1893.] [120–31]

_____. *Roughing It.* Hartford, Conn.: American Publishing, 1872. [44–48]

_____. *Some Thoughts on the Science of Onanism.* Privately printed, 1952. [68]

_____. "Speech at Seventieth Birthday Dinner." Supplement, *Harper's Weekly,* 23 December 1905. [381–82]

_____. "Speech on Sixty-seventh Birthday." *Mark Twain's Birthday.* Privately printed, 1903. [295]

_____. *The $30,000 Bequest and Other Stories.* New York: Harper, 1906. [36]

_____. *The Tragedy of Pudd'nhead Wilson and the Comedy of Those Extraordinary Twins.* Hartford, Conn.: American Publishing, 1894. [148–58]

_____. *A Tramp Abroad.* Hartford, Conn.: American Publishing, 1880. [69]

Sources

Clemens, Will M. *Mark Twain His Life and Work: A Biographical Sketch.* San Francisco: Clemens Publishing, 1892. [105–112]

DeVoto, Bernard, ed. *Mark Twain in Eruption: Hitherto Unpublished Pages about Men and Events.* New York: Harper, 1940. [289, 394–95, 398–400, 404]

Eggleston, George Cary. *Recollections of a Varied Life.* New York: Henry Holt, 1910. [408]

Ellis, Elmer. *Mr. Dooley's America.* New York: Knopf, 1941. [542]

Ellsworth, William Webster. *A Golden Age of Authors: A Publisher's Recollections.* Boston: Houghton Mifflin, 1919. [433–34]

Examiner (San Francisco). January 22, 29; March 19, 1893. [114–16]

Fisher, Henry W. *Abroad with Mark Twain and Eugene Field: Tales They Told to a Fellow Correspondent,* ed. Merle Johnson. New York: Nicholas L. Brown, 1922. [438–55]

Galaxy, The. New York: Sheldon. Vols. 9–11. [37–43]

Gillis, William R. *Gold Rush Days with Mark Twain.* New York: Boni, 1930. [505]

Goodwin, Charles C. *As I Remember Them.* Salt Lake City, Utah: Salt Lake Commercial Club, 1913. [430–31]

Gripenberg, Alexandra. *A Half Year in the New World (1888),* trans. and ed. Ernest J. Moyne. Newark, Del.: University of Delaware Press, 1954. [92]

Hare, Augustus J.C. *Story of My Life.* 6 vols. London: Geroge Allen, 1900. [285]

Harper, Henry. *House of Harper.* New York: Harper, 1912. [423–24]

Harper's Monthly. New York: Harper. Vol. 70 (1885). [80]

Henderson, Archibald. *Mark Twain.* London: Duckworth, 1911. [421–22]

Hollister, Wilfred R., and Harry Norman. *Five Famous Missourians.* Kansas City, Mo.: Hudson-Kimberly, 1900. [281–84]

James, George W. "Mark Twain and the Pacific Coast." *Pacific Monthly* 24 (August 1910): 115–32. [420]

Johnson, Merle. *Bibliography of Mark Twain.* New York: Harper, 1935. [30–35, 164]

———, ed. *More Maxims from Mark.* Privately printed, 1927. [322–67]

Lorch, Fred W. "Mark Twain in Iowa." *Iowa Journal of History and Politics,* 27 (1929): 408–456. [2–3, 6, 79]

Mark Twain Journal. Kirkwood, Mo.: Cyril Clemens. Vol. 17 (1974–75). [543]

Marquis, Don. *Chapters for the Orthodox.* New York: Doubleday, Doran, 1933. [509]

Matthews, Brander. *The Tocsin of Revolt and Other Essays.* New York: Charles Scribner's, 1922. [368]
Mentor, The. New York: Crowell Publishing, Vol. 12 (1924). [463–68]

New York *Times.* April 15, 1907. [396]
Niagara Book. Buffalo: Underhill and Nichols, 1893. [117]

Overland Monthly and Out West Magazine. San Francisco: Overland Monthly. Vol. 87 (1929). [473–77]

Pacific Outlook (Los Angeles). April 30, 1910. [414–17]
Paine, Albert Bigelow. *Mark Twain, A Biography.* New York: Harper, 1912. [425–29]
Phelps, William Lyon. "As I Like It." *Scribner's Magazine* 95 (1934): 432–35. [510]

Quackenbos, John B. "Mark Twain in an Emergency." *Century* 85 (1913): 637. [432]

Read, Opie. *Mark Twain and I.* Chicago: Reilly and Lee, 1940. [519–40]
Reader's Digest. Pleasantville, N.Y.: Reader's Digest Association. Vol. 31 (1937). [517]
Rice, Cale Young. *Bridging the Years.* New York: Appleton-Century, 1939. [518]
Rice, Clarence C. "Mark Twain as His Physician Knew Him." *The Mentor* 12 (May 1924): 48–49. [461–62]
Richards, P. "Reminiscences of Mark Twain." *Library Review* 4 (Spring 1933): 19–22. [507–508]
Rideing, William H. *Bookman* (New York) 31 (June 1910): 381–82. [418]

Simmons, Edward. *From Seven to Seventy: Memoirs of a Painter and a Yankee.* New York: Harper, 1922. [436–37]
Stewart, William M. *Reminiscences of Senator William M. Stewart of Nevada.* New York and Washington: Neale Publishing, 1908. [402]
Stoddardt, Alexander McD. "Twainiana." *The Independent* 68 (5 May 1910): 960–63. [409–413]

Ticknor, Caroline. *Glimpses of Authors.* Boston: Houghton, Mifflin, 1922. [435]
Twainian. Elkhorn, Wis.: Mark Twain Association of America. Vol. 2 (1940). [541]
Two Hundred After Dinner Stories as Told by Many American Humorists. New York: J.S. Ogilvie, 1902. [296–99]

Webster, Doris and Samuel. "Whitewashing Jane Clemens." *Bookman* (New York) 61 (July 1925): 531–35. [469–71]

Wiggin, Kate Douglas. *My Garden of Memory: An Autobiography*. Boston: Houghton, Mifflin, 1923. [457–58]

Wilson, Francis. *Francis Wilson's Life of Himself.* Boston: Houghton, Mifflin, 1924. [459–60]

Subject Index

Only stories are indexed, not contexts in which they were told. References are to entry numbers, not pages.

Mark Twain Laughing has been composed into type on a Compugraphic digital phototypesetter in eleven point Garamond with one point of spacing between the lines. Garamond was also used as display. The book was designed by Ed King at Hillside Studio, composed by Metricomp, Inc., printed offset by Thomson-Shore, Inc., and bound by John H. Dekker & Sons. The paper on which the book is printed carries acid-free characteristics and is designed for an effective life of at least three hundred years.

THE UNIVERSITY OF TENNESSEE PRESS : KNOXVILLE